Coping
with
Technological Change

Manik Kher is a UGC Research Scientist affiliated to the University of Pune. A Ph.D. in industrial sociology, she has been widely published in leading journals and newspapers and has previously authored five books: *From Shadows to Light: A Socio-legal Approach to Work Atmosphere* (1991); *Labour–Management Court Battles: The Manoeuvring Game* (1988); *Alienation from Work and Organization: Revisiting the Theory* (1988); *Conciliation and Adjudication Today* (1985); and *Profile of Industrial Workers* (1984).

Coping
with
Technological Change

MANIK KHER

Response Books
A division of Sage Publications
New Delhi/Thousand Oaks/London

First published in 1997 by

r

Response Books
A division of Sage Publications India Pvt Ltd
M–32 Greater Kailash Market–I
New Delhi 110 048

Sage Publications Inc
2455 Teller Road
Thousand Oaks, California 91320

Sage Publications Ltd
6 Bonhill Street
London EC2A 4PU

Published by Tejeshwar Singh for Response Books, typeset by Line Arts Phototypesetters, Pondicherry and printed at Chaman Enterprises, New Delhi.

Library of Congress Cataloging-in-Publication Data

Kher, Manik.
  Coping with technological change / author, Manik Kher.
    p. cm.
  Includes bibliographical references and index.
    1. Technological innovations—Management. I. Title.
  HD45.K47   1997   658.5'14—dc21   96–50326

ISBN: 0–8039–9354-4 (US-HB)   81–7036–599-6 (India-HB)
      0–8039–9366–8 (US-PB)   81–7036–612–7 (India-PB)

Sage Production Editor: Ritu Vajpeyi–Mohan

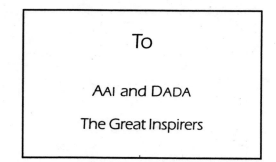

To

AAI and DADA

The Great Inspirers

Contents

7

Foreword

History has time and again proven that the process of change is inevitable in the progress of mankind. The ability of the human race to innovate has resulted in significant changes in our quality of lives.

The application of technology has, since the era of industrialization, brought about a radical transformation of society. The adoption of technology has had a significant bearing on human relations within an industrial organization. A company is recognized to be successful if it ably displays its ability to assimilate technological change without impinging on the harmony of human relations of its employees.

It is therefore appropriate that Dr Manik Kher has chosen to write on the subject of 'Coping with Technological Change' specially at a time when the ongoing economic reform process in India and the resultant liberalization have brought in their wake entirely new management styles and contemporary world-class technologies. At times like this, more than ever, it is essential that organizations appreciate the human resource management skills required to successfully handle the transformation of industry through one of its most critical periods. It is in this context that Dr Kher's analysis of the state of industrial relations in India serves as a useful reference for practitioners within the industry. In this book the role of training, union–management relationship and organization of work to create a 'technology friendly' work culture have been brought out explicitly by her. The organization of the various chapters is such that it allows the relevant issues to be dealt with at length and in a focused manner. The treatment of the subject is simple and holds the interest of the reader throughout the book.

I am sure that industry, students of management and the academia will find Dr Manik Kher's book useful in understanding the human impact of technological change within organizations. My best wishes for its success.

Bombay House
Fort, Bombay   **Ratan N. Tata**

Preface

Research of this kind requires wholehearted support from respondents and as such it can never be imposed on them. A researcher's findings are based on the data furnished by respondents and their honest sharing of work experiences with the investigator. However, barring a few notable exceptions, many managements had reservations on account of various apprehensions. 'What do we gain from wasting our time for you?' was the most common question. Despite my written assurances of maintaining organizational anonymity, they feared leaking out of information to their competitors. For some, fear of being exposed to the outer world was the root cause of denying permission. Whatever the reason, permission to conduct research was hard to come by. With one notable exception, almost all the public sector units did not respond to letters when approached for permission. I then had to visit some distant places merely for obtaining permission and revisit them for data collection at a later date.

During one such introductory visit, permission was granted to me orally by the Executive Director since the Managing Director was away. Six months later, when I went to commence my field work, a new Managing Director had assumed office. And due to the changed power equations, he disapproved of the Executive Director's decision to allow me to conduct research. Having travelled nearly 3,000 kilometres my tenacity and tact was put to the test. In another public sector company, the CEO had granted permission on the advice of a senior manager. However, four days later he withdrew it on the advice of another colleague!

It is normally believed that companies in the private sector are less bureaucratic and hence more easily approachable by researchers. This, however, turned out to be a misnomer. And multinational companies were found to be more secretive than Indian companies. The respondents in one MNC were apprehensive of their superiors' reactions to what they had stated to me. In one company, although I commenced data collection only after obtaining a written permission from the Corporate Head, the local CEO asked me to obtain another 'final approval' from the former on the collected data! Such experiences have only improved my patience and enriched my experience of group dynamics in industry. They have also taught me that your net has to be wide enough so as to make allowances for dropping a few 'catches'.

I am highlighting these problems not to cover up my shortcomings but only to stress the lack of research culture in industries. Despite these, I was very fortunate to obtain a good response from a few organizations. A couple of good CEOs not only valued my research and extended help in all possible ways but also gave me a 'royal' treatment. Even in those companies which were not so open and favourable to research, I happened to meet some good respondents who made my research meaningful. In order to honour their feelings, I cannot disclose their identity. Similar has been the case with the data they provided. However, all observations are based upon the grassroots data I collected.

This project was undertaken as the University Grants Commission Award in February 1991. It gave me a wider canvas, more variety in work and a tremendous sense of accomplishment. I am grateful to the Commission for giving me such a unique opportunity.

I am indebted to Mr Ratan Tata for gracing this book with his foreword. I have been greatly benefitted by friendly help and advice of Mr Biswanath Roy, Ms Freya Barua and Mr Y. B. Bhonsle. Mr Ranjan Kaul of Sage Publications responded encouragingly and made useful suggestions. My gratitude to all is inexpressible.

MANIK KHER

1

Technological Change and Industrial Relations: Analyzing the Nexus

Technological change is a sine qua non for not only the survival of business but also for maintaining its competitive edge and growth. Its cumulative effect reflects in industrial and socio-economic development. New technology does not merely and necessarily mean micro-electronics, automation and robotics. The term, as being used in the present study, is applied even to a new technique of producing the end product with a changed combination of the existing and newly acquired human and material resources. Such a broad coverage would bring within its purview not only the replacement of old machinery but also the modernization of work processes from low cost automation to highly capital intensive processes of full automation.

WHY MODERNIZATION?

Modernization or technological change is essential for many reasons. It brings about a refinement in the end product with more precision, better quality and consistency. As many of the skills are taken over by the automated work processes, the scope for human error is reduced. The management acquires a better control over the reduction of wastages and the efficiency of operators. Operating costs come down with the reduced cycle time of operations. Technological change brings about this effect only if all the resources—capital, raw material, machinery and labour—are utilized efficiently.

The decision to introduce new technology is largely, if not entirely, determined by the business environment, government policies and an overall market trend. Management has to be adept in sensing these changes and altering accordingly the product-mix or diversifying the business activity.

Technological change is not dictated totally by markets and economic policies. The advancement of technical knowledge culminates in technological sophistication and the innovation of new products. It is the spirit of entrepreneurship which transforms these innovations into a business activity. Technology provides various options to entrepreneurs and managers to work out a cost–benefit analysis with optimum profitability.

A change over to a new technology for any of the aforementioned objectives implies a reshuffle in the business operations. The most prominent change is on the shopfloor. Automation of processes makes certain manual skills redundant and renders manpower surplus in the Indian context. It cannot be cost-effective unless productivity is increased. Effects of technological change are felt on the organizational structure which requires a reorganization to suit business exigencies.

A change in work processes has to be complemented by a change in productivity norms. Any such change is not easy to accept and implement. Technology, therefore, to use Monger's[1] phrase, is an emotion-charged issue. It is unlikely that the change would not be regarded with suspicion by unions and resisted due to the potential skill-redundancy and unemployment. Technological change, therefore, has a direct nexus with industrial relations. This does not mean that the effect of change should be evaluated in terms of the number of work stoppages. Our objective in the forthcoming chapters is not to establish a one-to-one relationship between the two. This study aims at analyzing the entire process of technological change in the overall framework of industrial relations at the plant. It is founded on the conviction that if labour–management relations are cohesive, technological change will be smooth and effective. This cohesion is reflected in a wide range of activities from willingness to undergo training for new skills to a good work culture. Another parameter of cohesion is the management's sharing of information with the union and the latter's involvement and cooperation in various joint activities. Technological change cannot be successful if the middle management is not enthusiastically involved in it. This involvement should take place right from sharing of information about the decision of introducing new technology to their active participation in the reorganization of shopfloor activity and the management system.

Reorganization of the manufacturing activity is not successful unless there is open communication between the top and middle management, and middle management and operatives. Concomitantly there has to be communication and coordination across departments.

Indeed, successful implementation of technological change depends upon human relations at all levels.

The term industrial relations as used in the present study denotes human relations. It does not demarcate human resource management (HRM) and personnel and industrial relations management as is done in many industries. As per this differentiation, proactive issues of training, suggestion schemes, quality circles, and health camps are clubbed as HRM activities. Also included in this are recruitment and training of employees in the management cadre. By and large HRM or HRD activity is operated from the corporate office. Plant level issues pertaining to the daily and monthly rated employees are dealt with under the rubric of personnel management. The HRD cell does not exist merely at the corporate office. If established at the plant level, its activities include the proactive jobs outlined earlier. Issues of collective bargaining, disciplinary actions broadly of a reactive nature are looked after by the personnel management and industrial relations division. Such a distinction is wrong and is instrumental in creating a drift in management due to the status attached to functions on the basis of the type of interaction and the kind of employees involved.

The best possible course would be to treat all such functions as human resource management. It is not possible to establish a cause–effect relationship between technological change and human resource management. The fact, however, remains that various HRM issues affect the speed, quality and success of modernization. The following diagram highlights this relationship.

As has already been stated, the terms technological change and modernization have been used interchangeably in this

Nexus between Modernization and Issues in Human Resource Management

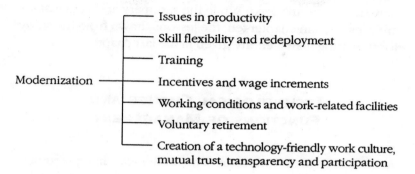

Modernization
— Issues in productivity
— Skill flexibility and redeployment
— Training
— Incentives and wage increments
— Working conditions and work-related facilities
— Voluntary retirement
— Creation of a technology-friendly work culture, mutual trust, transparency and participation

book. The chief objective of technological change is enhancement of productivity. This exercise, among other things, requires work-reorganization on the shopfloor. Chapters three and four focus upon it and analyze issues involved in the redeployment of labour. Manpower training assumes crucial importance while implementing technological change. Chapter five is devoted to this theme. Along with the above issues, incentives and wage increments occupy a prominent place in the collective bargaining process. Union approaches towards management vary across regions and industries. They are discussed in chapter six. Technological implementation cannot be successful unless a 'technology-friendly' work culture prevails in the organization. Various facets of work culture are analyzed in chapter seven. Irrespective of the legal constraints on manpower retrenchment during modernization, it is effected through the 'Golden Handshake'. Issues concerning this are presented in chapter eight. Financial stakes in the introduction of new technology compel the managements to involve workers in the production process and obtain their cooperation. The realization that the rift between the two will do more harm than good has ushered new trends of cooperation and a conscious effort to create trust and transparency in information-sharing. In chapter nine these new trends are analyzed. While the summary and conclusions are presented in chapter ten, the lessons drawn from the study for practising managers are given in the last chapter.

TECHNOLOGICAL CHANGE AND FUNCTIONS OF MANAGEMENT

At the outset, an introduction of technological change requires managerial skills in meticulously planning and scheduling for its implementation in phases. The management must also develop the infrastructure to sustain change both in production as well as service functions.

Technological change is basically designed by the project/process planning department in association with the industrial engineering and production departments. It involves a selection of an appropriate technology, designing of the shop layout, deciding capacity utilization, work-flow, manning of machines and preparing work norms. These are the initial basic tasks that planning and industrial engineering departments render.

Once the manning system is designed, it is the job of the personnel department to recruit or redeploy operatives in consultation with trade unions. In their effort to please the union (in order to maintain industrial peace) the personnel department makes many compromises, relaxes standards of discipline and is unable to check a number of unproductive practices. It is very unlikely, therefore, that the personnel department has a smooth relationship with other departments. It is possible to avoid this and it must be done in the interest of the organization.

While designing the shop layout, it is necessary to involve the maintenance management people. Water and electric connections, outflow of effluents have to be decided at the initial stage for facilitation of maintenance functions. However, maintenance is an ignored activity in many industries. Gaps in communication across departments and levels of hierarchy are not uncommon. Flaws in the management information system affect inter-departmental coordination and affect organizational efficiency.

Technological change reaps good results only if the work culture is conducive to change and people are enthusiastic about implementing new technology.

THE FRAMEWORK

The present study is aimed at studying the entire process of introducing and implementing technological change against the overall framework of human relations in industry. It is an inter-industry, inter-region comparative study. Table 1.1 gives an idea about the organizations covered in this study.

TABLE 1.1

The Coverage

Industry/Sector	Private	Public	Total
Steel	1 integrated steel 1 midi-steel	2 integrated steel	4
Textile	3	8	11
Engineering	6 (1 MNC)	1	7
	11	11	22

States: Andhra Pradesh, Bihar, Gujarat, Maharashtra, Tamil Nadu and West Bengal

21

The respondents were selected by a judgement sampling method and personal interviews. Quantitative data were collected from various sources and discussions were held with commissioners of labour, secretaries of chambers of commerce and mill owners' associations, professionals, academics and trade union leaders at the unit and state level in various regions.

The classical approach of researchers in social sciences has been that of case studies and presenting them as Factory A, B, C, etc. In the present book I have made a conscious effort to discard this approach by grouping the organizations industry-wise for analysis. Yet, examples of individual companies have been given whenever found appropriate. Thus the process of implementing technological change at both enterprise and industry levels has been presented.

Before analyzing the findings of this research, it would be pertinent to study the government policies towards technology adaptation. This is the subject matter of the next chapter.

REFERENCE

1. **R. F. Monger**, *Mastering Technology: A Management Framework for Getting Results*, The Free Press, 1988, p. 257.

2

Technological Adaptation: Perspectives and Issues

Technological change is not a recent or an unusual phenomenon. Ever since man mechanized a manual task in order to reduce drudgery, he has realized the value of technology. Benefits of technology have induced and motivated him to apply his creativity to continuously innovate and adapt new technology. Technology has not only reduced his fatigue but made possible more and better production at a reduced unit cost as also new products. It has further enabled mass production of goods and services which were the prerogatives of a privileged few. They are now within the reach of the previously deprived and the downtrodden.

While technology is a scientific phenomenon, its direction of use is largely a matter of government policy shaped by the prevailing economic situation and political ideology. In the case of India, the government approach has undergone a sea change over time. This will have to be understood in a historical perspective.

The modern factory sector in India emerged under the British rule in the latter half of the nineteenth century. However, it lacked local investment, entrepreneurship and participation due to complacency of the wealthy and the very fact that the country was under colonial rule. Industrial development under the British was planned to suit their political and economic exigencies. It neglected development of heavy industries. It is noteworthy, however, that way back in 1938 the Indian National Congress had emphasized the role of industrialization in economic development and appointed a National Planning Committee for the purpose. This committee had directed the creation of a public sector for basic and large-scale industries. This approach was later endorsed by the government of independent India in its Industrial Policy Resolution and the Industries (Development and Regulation) Act, 1951. Both of these are rooted in the Directive Principles of the Constitution enunciating the socialist pattern of society.

In pursuance of this ideology, the government not only created the public sector for the dual purpose of industrial development and employment generation but also focused on its protection from private competition by denying permission and fiscal incentives for the development of private enterprise. This policy was supported through the enactment of the Monopolies and Restrictive Trade Practices Act, 1969. In practice, however, its purpose got distorted as it was instrumental in generating corruption through the license and permit raj.

Another factor which hindered the adoption of new technology was the price control policy for commodities like steel, cement, coal, fertilizers and cotton textiles. It not only failed to generate internal profits necessary for technological upgradation, but also did not provide relief to the actual consumers. Bhagwati and Desai[1] candidly observe that

>...price control merely implied that (largely) public sector steel was being sold to (mainly) private sector users at controlled prices, whereas these users were under no obligation whatsoever to price their outputs on a cost-plus basis and hence price what the market would bear. The effect of such price control, therefore, was more to subsidize the user industries, enabling them to earn the profits which otherwise would have been caused by the producers of iron and steel (who were mostly in the public sector). This represented, therefore, a policy leading to loss of 'revenue' for the Government, without any real benefit (in terms of lower prices) accruing to the *final* consumers of products using iron and steel (p. 275).

The 'noble' objective of generating employment through the public sector in actuality resulted in overmanning of unskilled labour and incompetent technical personnel. Most of the public sector industrial projects suffered from 'extremely poor quality in general of the work, both from the point of view of economic cost and benefit analysis'.[2] Such a condition prevailed (as we shall see later) even at the time of my fieldwork in the public sector companies.

At the same time, government policies also evolved guiding principles regarding the choice of technology for industry. An appropriate Technology Cell was set up at the Ministry of Industrial Development for evolving technology conducive to local socio-economic conditions and a balanced regional economic development. It was, however, mainly concerned with the development of cottage industry. Government policies were also influenced by the debate on acceptance of intermediate technology as advocated by E. F. Schumacher.[3] The term 'intermediate' connotated a stage of technology, between the crude and highly sophisticated, suitable to local conditions. He also advocated a smaller size of industry for promoting production without worker displacement. However, intermediate technology has remained undeveloped till now. Attempts have been made to develop twelve spindle *charkhas* but widespread acceptance has been lacking in rural areas. Moreover, small may be beautiful as Schumacher envisioned, but what should be the size of smallness is still an open question. In the steel sector, in the sixties, there was a debate as to whether the government should encourage mini steel plants in the small sector. It was thought that mini steel plants (as also the small-scale industries in general) would save capital which is scarce. Hence, fiscal incentives were given to mini steel plants. Many of these, however, did not prove to be viable. S. S. Sidhu[4] observes that mini steel plants are viable only in conditions of

1. plenty of scrap supply;
2. adequate and cheap power supply; and
3. ready local market.

In the absence of all these, mini steel plants could not survive. In fact, as Sidhu notes, they remained 'mere steel scrap melting shops' unequipped with professional expertise.

As stated earlier, the government's protectionist approach towards the public sector had curbed private enterprise. In the steel sector, for instance, it denied permission for capacity expansion and modernization to the only integrated steel factory in the private sector. Price controls also denied generation of revenue needed for expansion.

The textile sector, too, was badly affected due to the licensing and price control policies of the government. The policy was evolved on the basis of four divisions in the textile sector, namely, composite mills, powerlooms, handlooms and khadi. The textile policy imposed many restrictions on the mill sector thereby denying to it opportunities for expansion, modernization and diversification. It was rooted in the Gandhian model of development encouraging handweaving and home spinning. The policymakers endeared it on the assumption of a labour surplus economy. Some spheres of production were reserved for the handloom sector. With a prejudice against use of power for looms, innovation of new technology was discouraged and hindered. Commenting upon the choice of appropriate technology for the textile sector, Bhagwati and Chakravarty[5] point out:

1. The fact that alternative techniques may have different impacts on quality and hence also export performance, was not seriously considered.

2. While computations of 'reinvestible' surplus were made for each technique, it was forgotten that similar computations would have to be made all the way, 'backwards' to get a complete answer: the reinvestible surplus may be higher in technique A than in technique B if we take only the final stage of production into consideration, but the ranking may reverse if both direct and indirect reinvestible surplus were taken into account.... The fallacy consisted in carrying over an argument, worked out at the macro level to the evaluation of a micro industry.

While a number of restrictions were imposed on the mill sector, the powerloom sector proliferated due to a number of fiscal concessions it enjoyed. Above all it managed to keep its labour costs low by escaping from a number of labour legislations. Incidence of labour exploitation had been rampant in this sector.

A scheme for the compulsory production of subsidized controlled cloth was introduced in 1964. Initially, 50 per cent of the production was earmarked for such production. The cloth was priced at Re. 1.50 per metre. From time to time this scheme underwent changes in terms of quality, quantity and price. The industry responded to these statutory requirements with escape routes of manufacturing poor and substandard cloth unacceptable to consumers. The highly subsidized mill-made cloth was found to provide unfair competition to handloom products and retarded the growth of this sector. Sickness of textile mills is sometimes related to this obligation of producing controlled cloth. The price control policy did not in any way promote the objective of making cheap cloth available to the masses. An analysis of the retail price-wise distribution of cotton cloth in 1977 showed that only 20.4 per cent of cloth distributed was in the price range below Rs 3 per metre.[6] Thus, the very policy of demarcation between the handloom, powerloom and mill sectors led to unhealthy competition as they posed a threat to each other's growth. The textile policy which aimed at protecting indigenous technology could neither increase employment nor boost cloth production nor fix the distribution at a low price. The victim of all these was the mill sector which was compelled into complacent with traditional, primitive and obsolescent technology. Continued losses, fear of closure and the eventual large-scale unemployment and pressures from trade unions compelled the government to take over sixteen composite textile mills in 1968. The remaining private sector mills are trying to diversify and produce for exports. They perforce have only recently launched the modernization programme when they could no longer continue with the old technology. The NTC mills, however, found it extremely difficult to revive in the wake of scarcity of funds and union resistance.

Similar also was the case with the engineering industry. For modernization, they either had to import technology or enter into collaboration with foreign engineering companies. However, till the policy of liberalization was initiated in 1985 and expedited since 1991, the licensing, price control policies and the Foreign Exchange Regulation Act posed many obstacles in techno-economic foreign collaborations and in accepting a market-oriented approach for growth.

As an overall effect of these policies, stagnation, low growth and inflation engulfed the Indian economy during the eighties. The per annum GDP growth rate decelerated from the average of 5.7 per cent in 1985–90 to 2.6 per cent in 1990–92. Foreign exchange reserves remained at a precarious level. Rising petrol prices, decline in remittances from the Middle East, fall in exports to industrialized countries which were facing recession hit the Indian economy very badly. Due to a very fragile balance of payments position, India had lost its credibility with the World Bank and the International Monetary Fund.

Having realized that its trade policies were not conducive to economic growth, the government initiated the liberalization process in 1985 by partially lifting curbs on imports. The new government which came to power in 1991, continued the liberalization programme initiated in 1985 and introduced a number of structural reforms. These were aimed at achieving the following:

1. a liberalized trade regime characterized by lower tariff rates and the absence of discretionary import licensing;

2. an exchange rate system which is free of allocative restrictions for trade;
3. a prudent and efficient financial system operating in a competitive market environment;
4. an efficient and dynamic industrial sector subject only to regulations relating to environment, security, strategic concerns, industrial safety, unfair trading and monopolistic practices; and
5. an autonomous, competitive and streamlined public enterprise sector for providing essential infrastructure, goods and services and the development of key natural resources and areas of strategic importance.[7]

Major structural reforms pertaining to the Export–Import Policy and New Industrial Policy were announced in July and August 1991. Through these policies there was a delicensing of a number of industries. Licensing is now compulsory only for fifteen types of items. The number of industries reserved for the public sector too have been reduced to six. Private initiative is now encouraged in the development of infrastructure like power, roadways, telecommunications, shipping and ports, airports and civil aviation, etc. Automatic approval is now given for technology transfer agreements and for 51 per cent foreign equity capital in industry. Foreign investment has been liberalized in thirty-five high priority industries.[8] These reforms are aimed at removing the stranglehold of the all pervading 'permit and licence raj'.

These measures, including price decontrol of industrially essential commodities like steel and cement, have encouraged industries to diversify their products and modernize their operations through import of technology or foreign collaboration in various ventures.

An overview of these developments highlights the transition in the very attitude towards technology. Acceptance of new technology irrespective of its mode through import of foreign collaboration has been encouraged.

Transition from old technology to new technology is bound to create issues on various counts, both at the individual and collective levels. At the individual level, this author found in her earlier work[9] that new technology, and automation in particular, created tension and alienation due to repetitiveness and deskilling. It also failed to provide a sense of accomplishment in work. Hence, the present study has been focused merely upon the effect on technology at the collective level.

Modernization of work operations involves change in work organization at the shopfloor, reduction in manual activity resulting in rendering of manpower surplus. The statutory restrictions on retrenchment of surplus employees and union resistance create the issues in absorption of this manpower through redeployment and training. These issues have wider implications for industrial relations.

TECHNOLOGICAL CHANGE AND INDUSTRIAL RELATIONS

The reason as to why technological change, regarded as an industrial relations problem according to Hyman (1988),[10] is 'the notion that technology is a managerial prerogative and that the role of industrial relations with respect to technical change is properly restricted to regulating its consequences in the work place but not its substance or direction. This view, in turn, is closely linked to an idea of technical development as an essentially unilinear and unidimensional process which is either interest neutral or closely identified with the interest of management. The consequence is the same: *there is in principle, nothing to negotiate*' (p.32).

In practice, however, trade unions do try to exert their influence on the potential consequence of new technology and in the process industrial relations are affected. Most of the studies on technological change have been focused on union resistance to change in a wide range of industries from printing, engineering, food, steel and textiles. We shall briefly present them here.

One of the pioneering works with a comparative approach is by L. C. Hunter, G. L. Reid and D. Boddy (1970)[11] carried out in the early sixties. This study focuses on three industries in Britain, namely, printing, steel and chemicals. The authors have covered such aspects as objectives of introducing technological change and the subsequent changes in skill content and the consequent adjustment problems at a collective level.

During the initial period of technological change in the printing industry, the objective of introducing new technology was not to reduce labour but to improve quality. Hence, problems associated with the large-scale redundancy or redeployment of labour were rare. In the chemical industry, as Hunter *et al.* note, technological change had not created any substantial change in manning patterns as the managements had evolved adjustment mechanisms by introducing inter-plant transfers and retraining of workers.

Fifteen years later, however, technological advancement in the printing industry created complicated issues in Britain. In *New Technology and Industrial Relations in Fleet Street* Roderick Martin (1981)[12] has presented case studies of technological change in British newspapers such as *The Times*, *Financial Times* and *The Mirror*. This change was dictated by poor financial position, poor cash flow and critical quality of printing. 'The introduction of new technology was seen as a way of reducing labour costs by reducing the number of employees and by reorganizing the remaining labour force. The basic objectives of the reorganization were increased flexibility in allocating labour and in working arrangements and the abolition of the piece work payment system' (p. 231). Although, the new printing system was supposed to be faster, more flexible and accurate, employers could not implement it successfully due to shortage of experienced technical staff. It resulted in staff turnover, exceptional escalation of salaries and a rift between technical and non-technical personnel.

UNION RESISTANCE

Technological change and union resistance are seen as a cause–effect nexus almost everywhere. As Paul Willman[13] notes

> Conflict over change is particularly likely where two condi-tions exist. On the one hand, cost cutting process innova-tions are more likely to generate resistance than product change: expanding sectors, where product rather than process change predominates are less likely to experience problems. On the other hand, spot contracting bargaining structures which transmit product–market volatility through to wages and employment, and which allow continuous union influence over job content are likely to generate conflict (p.247–48).

Willman differentiates between technological change with respect to product innovation and process innovation. He observes that 'Product innovation in performance maximizing areas might occasion a different form of resistance as employees could impose costs without immediate fear of job loss; process innovation designed to cut costs frequently involves the alternatives of acceptance or closure' (p. 259). He maintains that the economic, legal and political climate undercuts the capacity of unions to resist change. He refers to Slitcher *et al.* (p. 10)[14] who argue that trade union policies towards technological change depend on four main factors, namely

1. the proportion of union members affected by the change,
2. the economic condition of the industry or enterprise,
3. the nature of the technological change, and
4. its stage of development.

Trade union resistance, therefore, should be analyzed in the light of the existing level of technology and the extent of spade work done by the management to prepare the workforce mentally for accepting change. Despite the nature of resistance, technological change is compelling and pervasive. Willman notes in his concluding observations that technological change would affect trade union membership, and process change in particular would change the structure of craft unions. Such a change would force the unions (as in the case of EETPU—Electrical and Electronic, Telecommunications and Plumbing Union) to bend their stand by signing a no strike agreement in the high-technology industries (p.256). He further observes that the economic, legal and political climate would shape the overall trade union approaches towards the introduction of new technology.

It is not uncommon to find that union resistance to technological change impedes economic progress at the enterprise level. Commenting on trade union approaches in Britain, J. E. Mortimer[15] observes,

Unions contribute to industrial inefficiency by way of imposing limitations on output, insist on inflated manning scales, resist the introduction of new methods if the privileges of the existing workers are threatened and discourage or even prevent the employment of women in occupations for which they are physically suitable. Thus trade unions impede the optimum use of productive resources, including both men and equipment (p. 68).

Mortimer has cited a number of 'socially non-defensible' practices of trade unions. One of these is trade demarcation in which the unions insist that

a certain range of work is to be carried out exclusively by its members, irrespective of whether others could equally well do the same work; and conversely, the insistence by a union that its members should not be called upon to undertake certain tasks which fall outside their normal range of duties even though they may be perfectly capable of undertaking these other tasks (p. 71).

Over time, however, trade unions have come to realize the inevitability of accepting new technology. Structural changes brought on by modernization pose a challenge to trade union movement. Bamber[16] maintains that these changes pertain to:

1. capital intensiveness of industry, reduction in manual jobs and increasing thrust upon knowledge of workers,
2. growth of service sector,
3. increasing use of sophisticated information technology and fragmentation of organization of work, and
4. more employment in the smaller units.

These changes have affected union density in Japan, the USA and UK in the early eighties.

As noted before, technological change is now viewed positively by workers. This change is remarkable in Britain too. In his survey of 2,000 work places in the recent times (1987), W. W. Daniel[17] found that 'Technical change was generally popular among workers affected, but both shop stewards and full time union officers tended to support changes even more strongly than the ordinary workers they represented' (p. 260).

By and large, Daniel's survey showed that both workers and union leaders tended to be in favour of technical change at every stage. However, it was also found that where change led to loss of earnings, loss of jobs or less interesting work, there was more resistance. As these changes were associated with change in work organization, work practice and productivity agreements, they were not popular. Daniel has also compared the use of advanced technology in relation to employer and management structure. He observes that public services and nationalized industries are less likely to use advanced technology than private services and industries. As for the management structure, Daniel (p. 135) found that nationalized industries were more centralized in decision-making over the introduction of change. This centralization was associated with extensive involvement of full-time union officers in the introduction of technological change (57 per cent). Comparatively, consultation of union leaders in the private sector was on paper only (4 per cent) (p. 135).

The most noteworthy and immediate effect of technological change is the reorganization of work activity. It aims at introducing skill versatility in order to thereby reduce process time and manpower requirement. Daniel mentions production workers involved in maintenance work. These changes were introduced through productivity agreements. As we shall see later, experiences of Indian companies are similar.

That the introduction of new technology results in shrinking of employment is quite well-known. Daniel found this association stronger in the private sector. But the job reductions were not effected through dismissals. '(Employers) generally adjusted the size of their workforces through natural wastage, voluntary early retirement and voluntary redundancy scheme.... The people who suffered from these reductions were people seeking to enter employment rather than already employed in the workplaces introducing new technology' (p. 281).

EMPLOYEE PARTICIPATION IN TECHNOLOGICAL CHANGE

As the countries attain industrial maturity, they increasingly realize the importance of worker participation in decision-making. Daniel's findings, however, are negative. He candidly points out that 'The impression created by our findings is that the pervasive management approach to the introduction of change affecting manual workers was quite simply *opportunist*. When managers wanted to make changes, they simply set about introducing them, and if they could get away with it without consulting anyone they did so' (p.285).

In workplaces where unions were recognized and where there was initial resistance to the change or when some outcome of change was manifestly unfavourable, management consulted worker representatives. As mentioned earlier, consultation was rare in the private sector. In the nationalized industries, however, consultation practices were highly developed.

As in the UK, in Spain too, note Mamkoottam and Herbolzeimer (1991),[18] technological change is not a matter of negotiation between the management and unions. The authors have analyzed the reasons for employees and trade unions in Spain not resisting, in any significant fashion, the unilateral introduction of new technology in Spain. These are (*a*) the tradition of loyalty of Spanish employees towards their employers in return for job security from the state, (*b*) the remarkable ability of unions to come to agreements to face economic crises, and (*c*) a comparatively low union density.

The experience of worker participation in technological change in Germany, Italy, Japan, Sweden, UK and the USA has been analyzed in depth in an ILO study (1992).[19]

It covers (*a*) the methods of labour–management interaction on technological change, (*b*) the extent of workers' and unions' influence on the planning of technological change, and (*c*) the impact of labour–management interaction on the consequences of technological change, such as employment protection, income protection, work organization and retraining (p. 7). In Sweden, Germany, and France, the workers' right to participate in technological change has been legislated. In Italy, UK and the US, procedural rules for technological change have been formulated in collective agreement.

As for the workers' direct influence on planning of technological change, it seems to Ozaki (see note 19) to be limited in most countries with the exception of Sweden where workers have been able to exert the most far-reaching and direct influence on the planning of technological change (p.15). However, it varies across enterprises.

In cases in which labour–management cooperation has been practised only in compliance with the Co-determination Act, workers reportedly tend to complain that the information provided by the management is so scanty and so belated, and the management so unwilling to listen to the unions' views, that the subsequent negotiations do not have any real effect (p. 16).

In the UK, technology agreements have mostly been confined to job surety, payment for change and guarantees of union membership. Unions have had little influence on investments in new technology or concerning the type and extent of technology to be introduced, although they may have had some influence on the speed of introduction of new technology. In the US the ILO study reports, direct union influence on the planning of technological change seems virtually non-existent in the machine tool industry. In Japan too, union influence on decisions concerning new technology has been limited. The study points out that the choice of new technology has never been altered in any significant way because of requests from the unions.

As mentioned earlier, new technology has a labour saving effect. The ILO study notes that in Japan, Sweden and the US there does not seem to have been any significant development of special arrangements for protecting job security in the context of the introduction of new technology. Nevertheless, the study notes the spread of concession bargaining in the US. It involves 'improvements in job security as a *quid pro quo* for concessions by unions on wages'. For instance, the American Airlines extended lifetime job guarantees to existing workers and lowered the pay of new recruits during the 1983 negotiations. Instead of employment guarantees, Ford and General Motors provided for income support and redeployment for workers displaced by technological change or subcontracting of work. In Italy, the 'principle of avoiding compulsory redundancy resorting to early retirement, recruitment freeze, voluntary redundancy and transfer is fairly well established'. In Germany and the UK, although limited, new negotiated clauses in agreements for protection of employment have emerged. They do not preclude dismissals but relegate them as a means of last resort. In the UK, the frequent provision in settlements has been that job losses will be not through dismissals but by voluntary redundancy and natural wastage. Daniel's study, too, (note 17 p. 236) confirms this method of employment shrinkage. In Japan, the system of employment has reduced the need for special measures to protect employment when new technology is introduced.

WORK ORGANIZATION

The impact of new technology is most immediately reflected in the work organization on the shopfloor. The ILO study has dealt with this aspect in detail.

Skill rigidity introduced by the Taylorist system of work organization is unsuitable to meet the demands of new technology and market forces. A flexible work system facilitates product diversification. It is noteworthy that in Germany, the unions exerted pressure on the management for creating integrated jobs and team work among the highly skilled workers. On the contrary, the British and American unions have focused their efforts on defending rights attached to particular jobs in the context of rigid divisions of labour (p. 29). As a pleasant departure, in Italy, however, there has been a cooperative endeavour in work organization by labour and management. They have recast the traditional divisions of labour with a view to increasing autonomy, personal discretion, decision-making power and polyvalence. Such a cooperative system existed in the seventies. In the eighties, due to the accelerating pace of technological change and structural adjustments, the initiative on work organization seemed to have shifted from trade unions to management with a view to coping with requirements for increasing productivity.

In Japan, as the ILO study notes, there is an increasing thrust on involving individual workers through their work groups rather than through their unions.

Despite such cooperative systems, as has been observed in the study, it is difficult to draw any definite conclusions regarding

workers' influence on the final decisions of the management. The study, therefore, tries to draw inferences on the basis of certain tendencies. In Sweden, for instance, the joint project groups on new forms of work fosters the creation of broad work roles and granting of greater autonomy to work groups. The Swedish Working Environment Fund created through public policy even gives financial assistance to such semi-autonomous work groups. These have considerable technical and administrative autonomy. Similarly, in Germany, the trade unions have pressurized the management to provide training and job enrichment to workers and introduce skill flexibility.

In sum, the ILO study has shown that '...labour relations (namely, negotiations, consultation and other forms of labour–management interaction) influence the process of technological change both directly (that is, through the participation of workers and unions in the formulation of plans for changes and in decisions concerning their implementation) and indirectly (that is, by determining the consequences the changes are allowed to produce)'. In the ultimate analysis, the study observes that direct influence has been increasing, thereby influencing the selection of new technology and the pace and means of its introduction.

EFFECTS OF NEW TECHNOLOGY ON EMPLOYMENT

Technological change inevitably affects the patterns and levels of employment. Therefore, the ILO had adopted a tripartite declaration that multinational enterprises, while investing in developing countries, should adapt technologies to the needs and characteristics of the host countries. The impact of technological change has remained very controversial.

Sophisticated technology normally means use of computers and micro-electronics. Its likely impact on employment in India has also been discussed by the veteran trade union activist and thinker Bagaram Tulpule (1986).[20] He maintains that 'computerisation and automation will lead us to "jobless growth".' Based on statistical analysis K. J. Joseph's (1995)[21] study shows that the employment-producing potential of the electronics industry has been decreasing over time. It ranked fourth in 1976–77 and more than three persons were required to produce an output of one lakh rupees. Today, the industry ranks fourteenth and requires only one-sixth of the manpower (as compared to 1976–77) to produce the same output. This situation is attributable to the change in technology and increasing automation. Virmani, too (1990)[22] questions the appropriateness of transfer of technology from the point of view of its employment potential.

In a study conducted during the late seventies, Usha Dar examined the general impact of multinational enterprises on employment in India[23] and observed that

The share of multinational enterprises in overall employ-ment in the country is very insignificant, and it is also not substantial when viewed in terms of the employment in the organised private sector.... There are certain products which are being produced only by multinational enterprises in the country and therefore they are responsible for the entire direct employment in the industry.

Dar observes that though both multinational enterprises and Indian companies have similarly structured pay scales, the promotion opportunities in the former are faster and this is likely to have a major psychological impact upon the employees of the Indian companies.

That technological change reduces employment potential is very obvious. Does this mean that we should not opt for technological sophistication and modernization of the existing work process? The benefits of modernization are widely known. Although the immediate effect of new technology is reflected in the reduction of jobs, in the long run even the poor and the masses share the benefits.

The first and foremost requirement of any business is that it should be profitable. Employment generation can never be the sole objective of any business. In order to expand and be efficient and profitable, businesses should continuously re-engineer and adapt to new technology and new techniques of management. Reduction of jobs, since inevitable in this process, has to be tackled in different ways. Government policies should encourage the emergence of new industries where the unemployed can be absorbed. Trade unions and social organizations too should come forward to start business activities complementary to the main businesses. For instance, the retrenched employees can set up ancillary units and take up jobs subcontracted by the principal business organization. Moving towards efficiency, quality and cost effectiveness is the need of the hour. There is, therefore, no substitute to modernization and automation of the work processes.

The impact of technological change on employment is indirect. With its hope of wider market and increased profits, technological change encourages entrepreneurs to invest in various industries. An atmosphere of enthusiasm is created by change which will ultimately absorb more labour in these industries and their ancillary units.

TRADE UNION RESPONSES IN INDIA

Trade union approaches in India are guided by the tripartite 'Model Agreement' arrived at during the 15th session of the Indian Labour Conference in 1957. It laid down that there should be no retrenchment on account of technological change. It required the employers to provide workers with suitable alternative jobs in the same establishment or under the same employer. The workload of the worker was required to be assessed by experts and compensated with improved earnings and working conditions. This approach has, in effect, delayed modernization mainly in the public sector. As stated earlier, with the onset of liberalization, government policy has now become flexible and more favourable towards technological change. Over time trade union leaders too seem to have realized the importance and inevitability of technological change. In a seminar organized by the ILO-ARTEP in 1987, while recognizing the need for modernization, they emphasized the issue of employment generation.

Studies by Indian authors are, by and large, focused on union responses to new technology. K. B. Akhilesh *et al.* (1989)[24] presented six case studies in a paper titled 'Technological Change: Management Initiatives and Trade Union Response'. The management of organizations in their study seemed to have taken workers for granted while introducing new technology. The management thinking was that by providing some ex-gratia monetary benefits they would be able to overcome the resistance of the trade union. 'This "buying" approach failed miserably in getting active cooperation and support of the workmen. The purpose of introducing the technology for better quality and improved productivity was defeated and there was a failure of technology in terms of acceptance and use', note the authors. Lack of management efforts in creating awareness about new technology was one of the major causes of failure in the implementation of new technology.

Ranabir Samaddar (1995)[25] takes an extreme and biased view against new technology and with his few case studies in the newspaper industry tries to establish that new technology is a weapon in the hands of the management to deunionize workers. As I will analyze in chapter eight, the reasons for deunionization are quite different. Most importantly, management adopts new technology for better and higher economic returns than merely to weaken unions. Other Indian authors like Virmani (note 22) and Tulpule and Datta (1995)[26] too have examined the factors motivating the management's option of new technology.

The role of trade unions in modernization has been discussed by Mamata Roy (Chaudhuri).[27] She points out that after 1985, the rate of employment in the banking industry has been declining. But it has nothing to do with micro electronic (ME) technology. She raises a pertinent question as to whether resistance to ME technology from the bank unions would be able to maintain the employment rate (p. 347). She concludes that

> There is no reason why with...problems [of] very high staff costs and a dwindling surplus, Indian banks will not adopt a drastic manpower utilization plan like the one announced by the railways. Thus resistance to technical modernization on the grounds of curtailment may lose much of its appeal. Instead, the overburdened worker may become keen to get technological help (p.356).

With managements aggressively pursuing modernization, trade unions have by and large had to come to terms with it and the exigencies of the situation will leave them no option but to cooperate with managements in implementing technological change in the future. The chapters that follow will analyze the experiences of modernization of various companies covered in this study.

REFERENCES

1. **Jagdish N. Bhagwati** and **Padma, Desai**, *India: Planning for Industrialization*, Oxford University Press, 1970.
2. **Supra**, p. 158.
3. **E. F. Schumacher**, *Small is Beautiful*, Radha Krishna, 1977.
4. **S. S. Sidhu**, *The Steel Industry in India: Problems and Perspective*, Vikas, 1983, pp. 96–98.
5. **Jagdish N. Bhagwati** and **Sukhmoy Chakravarty**, 'Contributions to Indian Economic Analysis: A Survey in *The American Economic Review*, Vol. LIX No. 4, September 1969, p. 23.
6. Table 7 on p. 27, *Commerce*, 13 October, 1979.
7. Budget speech of the Finance Minister, July 1991.
8. The Economic Survey 1995–96, *The Economic Times*, 28 February 1996.
9. **Manik Kher**, *Alienation from Work and Organization: Revisiting the Theory*, Indus, 1988.
10. **Richard Hyman** and **Wolfgang Streeck**, *New Technology and Industrial Relations*, Basil Blackwell, 1988.
11. **L. C. Hunter, G. L. Reid** and **D. Boddy**, *Labour Problems of Technological Change*, George Allen and Unwin, 1970.
12. **Roderick Martin**, *New Technology and Industrial Relations in Fleet Street*, Oxford 1981.
13. **Paul Willman**, *Technological Change, Collective Bargaining and Industrial Efficiency*, Clarendon Press, 1986.
14. **S. H. Slitcher**, *et al.*, *The Impact of Collective Bargaining on Management*, Brooking Institute, 1960.
15. **J. E. Mortimer**, *Trade Unions and Technological Change*, Oxford University Press, 1971.
16. **Greg Bamber**, 'Technological Change and Unions' in *New Technology and Industrial Relations*, (eds.) Richard Hyman and Wolfgang Streeck, supra 10.
17. **W. W. Daniel**, *Workplace Industrial Relations and Technical Change*, Frances Pinter, 1987.
18. **Kuriakose Mamkoottam** and **Emil Herbolzeimer**, 'Human Resource Implications of New Technology: A Case Study of Automobiles in Spain' in *Indian Journal of Industrial Relations*, Vol. 26, No. 3, January 1991 pp. 205–226.

19. **Muneto Ozaki**, (ed.) *Technological Change and Labour Relations*, I.L.O., 1992.
20. **Bagaram Tulpule**, 'Computers, Industrial Development and Workers', in *Economic and Political Weekly*, Vol. XXI, No. 48, 28 November, 1986, pp. M-110-114.
21. **K. J. Joseph**, 'Output, Growth, Technology and Employment' in *New Technology and the Workers' Response* (ed.) Bagchi A. K., Sage, 1995 pp. 123–44.
22. **B. R. Virmani**, 'Automation and Changing Technologies: Issues and Concerns for Manpower Planning and Industrial Relations', *Indian Journal of Industrial Relations*, Vol. 25, No. 44, April 1990, pp. 323–34.
23. **Usha Dar**, *The Effects of Multi-national Enterprises on Employment in India*, I.L.O. Working Paper No. 9, 1979.
24. **K. B. Akhilesh**, *et al.*, Technological Change: Management Initiatives and Trade Union Response (unpublished draft) 1989.
25. **Ranabir Samaddar**, 'New Technology at the Shopfloor Level: The Story of Deunionization in Some Indian Newspapers' in *New Technology and the Workers' Response*, (ed.) Bagchi A. K., supra 21.
26. **Bagaram Tulpule** and **R. C. Dutta**, 'New Technology: Productivity, Employment and Workers' Response' in *New Technology and the Workers' Response* (ed.) Bagchi A. K., supra 20.
27. **Mamata Roy (Chaudhuri)**, 'Indian Banks, Information Technology and Bargaining' in supra 21.

3

Technological Change and its Implementation

Technological change is a multi-pronged process. It requires a continuous re-engineering of systems and processes. This means that on the one hand it is necessary to adapt to new processes which are cost-effective, and on the other hand change the product-mix and diversify so as to survive the changing market economy.

In the companies under study both these aspects of modernization went hand in hand. There were changes in both products and work processes. Across industries and sectors there were variations in the process of modernization.

In order to circumvent some government policies, some private industries designed their product-mix so as to escape price controls. Thus in steel, they switched to manufacturing high carbon special steels and in the textile industry, they started exporting grey yarn or introduced textiles of superfine quality. The modernization process in different industries covered in this study has been presented in Table 3.1. Improving labour productivity by reducing manpower and moving into tax-free zones of backward regions was another option to improve competitiveness. The industry was compelled to run its loss-making units due to the statutory restrictions on plant closure, layoff and retrenchment.

The long-awaited governmental policy of liberalization set in motion the process of modernization which, at the time of this study was underway on a big scale in both the private and public sectors. However, years of stagnation drastically affected the process of modernizing the public sector. The bureaucracy too contributed to delays in modernization. We shall now analyse this process sector and industry-wise.

STEEL

The Steel Development Fund created in April 1979 by the government provided an impetus for modernizing the integrated steel company in the private sector. A huge sum of 100 crores was made available to it from this fund. As soon as the company obtained this facility it engaged a private consulting firm to prepare a feasibility report on modernization. Following the committee's recommendations, the modernization

TABLE 3.1

Types of Modernization	Industries			Advantages
	Steel	Engineering	Textile	
Product change	Flat products	New models of vehicles	New varieties of cloth of a superfine quality	Improved labour productivity Better quality and consistency Better working coditions.
	Special steel	Modification of design of products		Higher precision. Reduction in process time. Higher consistency Reduction in cost of living
		Total dismantling of the old product (e.g., from paper-coated cables to jelly-filled cables)		
Process change	From ingots to continuous casting	Change in welding technology	Open end spinning eliminating some of the earlier stages of inter frames	Reduction in energy consumption Reduction in re-work, wastages.

From open hearth process to oxygen steel-making

Low cost automation to reduce fatigue and improve productivity

High cost automation through introduction of CNC machines and Flexible Manufacturing systems

High speed looms

programme was launched in phases. Phase I was directed at the replacement of the outdated and uneconomic process of making steel in steel melting shop with oxygen steel making by installing an LD converter shop. Along with this, some improvements in the blast furnaces too were effected. The first phase of modernization was completed expeditiously within two years. It was aimed at increasing productivity, improving product quality and reducing energy consumption and operating costs. Modernization in the first phase resulted in a marginal increase in saleable steel by about 7 per cent.

Phase II sought to improve the blast furnace for further reducing energy consumption through a lower coke consumption rate thus leading to higher productivity. The facilities comprised a sinter plant with an increased capacity of producing sinter by enhancing the blast furnace burden from 40 to 65 per cent, a raw material bedding and blending yard to ensure a consistent mixture of the input for sinter, a new coke oven battery with stamp charging facility to improve coke strength and a bar and rod mill with a high capacity of output.

Phase III was aimed at upgrading the flat product mills. The old mills were proposed to be retired in phases and the thrust was towards making special steels (which prior to decontrol of steel prices lay outside the controlled category) having a great export potential. Thus modernization in the integrated steel plant in the private sector was aimed at adopting an energy-saving, cost-effective method of making steel. The fuel rate of 11.98 M.K. Cal./t. (million kilo calorie per tonne of saleable steel) in Phase I was proposed to be brought down to 8.91 in Phase III. The ratio of steel ingots to continuous casting was being changed. While the proportion of ingots would reduce from 84.3 per cent in Phase I to 57.2 per cent in Phase III, the proportion of continuous casting would increase from 15.7 per cent to 42.8 per cent during the same period. An increased thrust was placed on the production of flat products that had a high profit margin. The percentage of flat products was being raised from 24.8 per cent to 37.1 per cent of the total production. The percentage decreases in non-flat products were from 34.1 in Phase I to 29.3 in Phase III. These in the case of various semi-finished saleable steel products were respec-tively from 41.1 per cent to 33.6 per cent.

MODERNIZATION IN THE
PUBLIC SECTOR STEEL PLANTS

Integrated steel plants in the public sector came under the umbrella of the Steel Authority of India Ltd (SAIL). They are situated in Bihar, West Bengal and Madhya Pradesh, areas which have rich deposits of natural mineral resources essential for making iron.

Most of the SAIL plants came into existence in the early fifties with technical know-how and collaboration obtained from the UK and the erstwhile USSR. Although started with the best technology available at that time, they were soon afflicted by bureaucracy, complacency, neglect and a slow deterioration of efficiency. Labour militancy coupled with violence and destruction of plant and machinery further worsened the situation making these plants economically unviable. The report of the Bureau of Industrial Costs and Prices ('Comprehensive Study of Integrated Steel Plants in India and International Cost Competitiveness', hereinafter referred to as BICP Report)[1] noted that there was a deterioration in the quality of major inputs, technological parameters and cost parameters in comparison to international practices and other integrated steel plants in India. It reiterated the need to improve productivity of blast furnaces, reduce coke rate and improve energy consumption and other factors related to hot metal quality.

Product-Mix

Product-mix is an important determinant of profitability and competitiveness of any business. In the steel industry changing the product-mix is a time-consuming and very expensive task. Hence, it is essential that the product-mix is designed with great vision and care.

The product-mix of one of the SAIL plants covered in this study was faulty. Basically designed to cater to the needs of the public sector and the requirements of the national economy envisaged in the late fifties, the product-mix of 30 per cent semi-finished steel (which had no market value) and 70 per cent finished steel was faulty. Thus an annual net loss of Rs 3.6 crores was built in even at 100 per cent capacity utilization at the time of the inception itself. The faulty product-mix coupled with the faulty pricing policy had pushed this public sector integrated steel plant into deeper and deeper economic losses. Various factors responsible for losses are detailed in what follows.

Faulty Pricing Policy

Being the principal supplier to the public sector, the manufactured steel products were sold at controlled and low prices which were not commensurate with the escalation of the cost of inputs. The major cost increases were with respect to landed costs of raw materials, energy inputs such as furnace oil and other liquid fuels, labour cost, refractories and spares. The average cost of products surpassed its selling price with a large gap of nearly Rs 1,000 per tonne. This gap was never bridged. The cost of production was one-and-a-half times more than the selling price.

Shortage of Raw Material Inputs

This public sector plant did not have captive mines for nearly twenty years since inception and had to depend upon Coal India Ltd. for its coal requirements. However, Coal India Ltd. failed to supply good quality coal as per the norms agreed upon: the ash content was 3.8 per cent higher than the commitment made. The coal of high ash content spoilt the washery. The ash content had never been below 20 per cent. It may be mentioned here that one per cent increase in ash content gives rise to 1.3 per cent ash in coke which increases the coke rate in the blast furnace by 40 kg per tonne of hot metal and decreases production of hot metal by 3 per cent. The supply of coal was also very inadequate, due to which production was held up. Moreover, losses were further compounded with the resultant damage to the equipment.

In view of the shortage and poor quality of domestic coal, the company under study began importing coal. The percentage of imported coal to total coal had been increasing over the years. It had increased from 9.79 per cent in 1985–86 to 38.67 per cent at the time of fieldwork.

Scarcity of Energy

Steel production had suffered also due to shortage of electricity. The company was dependent upon the State Electricity Corporation for its requirement of electric power other than its own meagre internal support of four generators. Even after installing its own captive power plant in 1987, the company continued to purchase power from the State Corporation.

However, its supply was irregular. Similarly, unequal supply of gaseous fuel to coke ovens, soaking pit and rolling mills had damaged the plant equipment. While the machinery in the mills deteriorated due to this idle state, coke ovens were damaged with depletion in oven pushes. As an overall effect, the rated capacity of the plant declined considerably. The government did not make the desired investment for preventive maintenance and revitalization of the equipment, not to speak of its modernization.

Poor Industrial Relations

One of the most important reasons preventing the government from making huge investments in plant modernization was poor industrial relations. An anarchic situation prevailed in the company. As noted by its erstwhile general manager, by the early seventies, the plant had reached an unbelievable stage. Employees behaved the way they liked and work stoppages and refusals to work were very frequent. Many workers left their jobs incomplete much before the scheduled shift hours. Rarely did the executives dare to take disciplinary action against those involved in pilferage, theft and mischief for fear of being '*gheraoed*' (wrongful physical confinement) by workers. Lack of maintenance and cleanliness caused the machinery to fall into disrepair. Besides, planned absenteeism leading to an 'artificial' need for overtime in connivance with colleagues and supervisors and the blatant refusal of job flexibility pushed the plant into sickness beyond revival.

Many work stoppages were politically motivated. The reason-wise break-up of loss of man-days was available only for the decade of the eighties. It showed that the percentage of strikes due to political reasons varied from 80 to 97 per cent.

Due to the combined effect of poor industrial relations, obsolete technology, faulty product-mix and pricing policy the plant under study had accumulated losses of over Rs 700 crores by 1990.

Lethargic Attitude of Revival

After decades of continuous setbacks, the government realized that technological obsolescence and high operating costs due to use of petrofuel in the energy-intensive open hearth process were no longer viable and would not help the company recover from its longstanding industrial sickness. It was in 1979 that the modernization plan was proposed and the British Steel Corporation was commissioned to prepare a feasibility report. That the conceptualization itself took nearly four years from 1980 to 1984 reflected the typical functioning of a public sector organization. It is noteworthy that within the same period the private sector integrated steel company had not only obtained a feasibility report but also commissioned its LD converter. In the public sector, however, nearly a decade was spent in consulting, reconsulting and obtaining second and third opinions of different consultants on the modernization proposals.

The proposal submitted by the British Steel Corporation was examined by an expert committee appointed by SAIL, the governing authority. It recommended additional facilities for achieving a higher level of production than that projected by the British Steel Corporation. Despite approval by the Board, SAIL invited the Japan Iron and Steel Federation to evaluate plant operations and examine the feasibility of modernization. They too endorsed the proposal submitted by the British Steel Corporation. An investment proposal for the first phase of technological upgradation was finalized by SAIL. Once again, this proposal, too, was examined by various government agencies before forwarding it to the Public Investment Board (PIB). Even after the PIB gave a clearance of a paltry sum of

Rs 25 crores (out of an estimated cost of Rs 1,256 crores) for modernization, another consulting body, MECON, was assigned to prepare a detailed project report in 1984. This report was reviewed by the British Steel Corporation. Thus it can be seen how the government machinery functions with hesitation and the lack of faith in its own consultants. Even when the final approval was accorded by the government in September 1987, the PIB did not agree to release the budgeted amount. After further negotiations, the contracts with global agencies, namely, Japan, Britain and the erstwhile USSR were finalized in February 1989. This entire process only highlights the inordinate delays created by the inbuilt bureaucracy which is not geared to catching up with the very pace of rapidly changing modern technology.

The estimated time schedule for completion of the process of production was four years after the finalization of the conceptual scheme in 1979. Even at the time of this study in December 1991, the process of modernization with Russian collaboration was still underway. The political upheaval in the USSR further delayed the project and even at the time of writing this report modernization was still behind schedule.

During fieldwork, this researcher had the opportunity to attend a high level executives' meeting to review the progress of the modernization process. The discussion highlighted a tremendous lack of coordination between those directly associated with production and the personnel executives. The latter could not explain the criteria adopted for assessing the manpower requirement. When new technology eliminates certain stages of production and skills, manpower planning is required to be done skill and job-wise depending upon the technological requirements after modernization. This, however, had not been done.

As the process of technological upgradation in this public sector steel plant was behind schedule, the researcher had no alternative but to study the state of affairs at the time of fieldwork and earlier, including the proposed change and the related aspects of industrial relations.

As energy constituted the major item of cost, important schemes to conserve energy were proposed to be taken up. Some of these included cold blast insulation in all four blast furnaces for reduction in the drop of cold blast temperature, incorporation of total heat input indicator in open hearth furnace for maintaining a standard thermal regime in the furnace and enrichment of calorific value of gaseous fuels. The principal objective of modernization was stated to be adoption of a fuel-efficient technology. The overall specific energy consumption was proposed to be reduced from 8.7 G-Cal per tonne to 6.9 G-Cal per tonne. It was aimed at achieving liquid steel capacity of 1.876 million tonne per annum (MTPA) and raising saleable steel production from 0.824 MTPA to 1.506 MTPA. The product-mix, too, was proposed to be changed.

TECHNOLOGICAL CHANGE IN THE PRIVATE SECTOR MIDI-STEEL PLANT

The process of making steel in this plant differs totally from the integrated steel plants mentioned earlier. Steel, in this company, was made by heating and melting the steel scrap in an electric arc furnace. After attaining the required metallurgical compositions for different grades of steel, the liquid steel was converted into a solid form of blooms. These blooms were then passed on to a wire rod mill for re-rolling into thin and long products of different sizes. Hence modernization in this plant was two-dimensional; in the steel melt shop and wire rod mill.

Steel Melt Shop (SMS)

The ladle refining furnace (LRF) was made by dismantling one of the four arc furnaces. The LRF was used for refining the arc furnace liquid metal to improve the quality of the alloy and special steels and save electric energy. The basic production process comprised segregation and mixing of steel scrap according to different metallurgical qualities, feeding them into a furnace, passing the liquid metal through the LRF for refining and decarbonization and then finally to the bloom caster.

The biggest advantage of this technology was the cycle time reduction from three hours per heat to one-and-a-half hours. The scrap pre-heating system of the UHPF and its fume exhaust could re-cycle the energy which could be re-used for preheating the scrap. The electricity and electrode consumption too has reduced considerably. While the production of billets and blooms increased by 93 per cent after modernization, the billets output per employee increased by 91 per cent. The electricity and electrode consumption came down respectively by 37 and 39 per cent.

Wire Roll Mill (WRM)

The work process in WRM involved receiving the billets manufactured in the SMS department from the billet yard and re-rolling them in a steel coil of 5.5 mm diameter to 2.5 mm diameter, raw corner squares and flat bars. For changing the diameter requirements, prior filling adjustments were required to be made. These were known as section change, involving skilled manual jobs. The time required for section change varied according to the size of the diameter of the required output.

The billets received from the billet yard were charged into a billet re-heating furnace from where the rolling was done automatically. The rolled products were then sent for inspection and further sent to the coil yard for dispatch.

Although rolling of coils has always been an automated process, further intensive automation was introduced in 1982. The jobs of lifting billets and feeding them on to the rolling table, which were earlier done manually, were now mechanized. There was a simultaneous change of the process route of rolling of steel. Modification in shop layout and reduction in roughing stands had resulted in speedier operations, higher output and a better quality of coils. The cooling bed, where hot coils were brought down to room temperature was also modified. This had improved the straightness of bars. As an overall gain of automation in WRM, the percentage of cobbles (i.e., defective coils which are rejected) declined tremendously. The production of rolled products increased due to automation by 48 per cent. The wire rod output per employee increased by 53.5 per cent. This rise in productivity was also due to reduction in manpower by 31 per cent. By and large new technology reduces energy input requirements and thus is cost-efficient. In WRM the monthly saving was up to Rs 2.5 lakhs due to reduction in the consumption of electricity and other fuels. Automation in WRM boosted plant utilization and production.

The private sector companies do not waste time and resources in decision-making. Their entrepreneural drive to excel and stay ahead of market competition pushes away all bureaucratic ways of decision-making. Hence despite suspension of operations and lock-out for 13 months in 1983–84, the modernization programme was successfully commissioned without much delay.

It is the drive to steer and stay ahead in the face of stiff competition that leads companies to re-engineer their systems, continuously upgrade the product-mix and improve quality cost-effectively. In the private sector, in both the engineering and textile industries researched in this study, this marked urge for continuous improvement was noticed.

A GREENFIELD PUBLIC SECTOR COMPANY

The researcher also covered an integrated steel plant in the public sector on the eastern coast of India. Commissioned in August 1992, the plant has a strategic location and the most modern technology. Its layout and major production facilities for iron and steel machinery were characterized by a high level of technological sophistication incorporating energy-saving and pollution-free systems.

The present study is essentially about the transition from the old technology to new. There was no question of such transition in this Greenfield plant. Yet it was selected for this study in order to learn the current technological developments. It was learnt that the management had evolved new management systems and practices in order to avoid the mistakes and drawbacks experienced in other public sector steel plants. By keeping the optimum level of manning, higher standards of labour productivity were achieved. Skill flexibility was being inculcated from the very beginning. The researcher has examined the way in which this was being done in the next chapter as well as chapter five.

MODERNIZATION IN THE ENGINEERING INDUSTRY

Compared to the steel industry, the engineering industry, especially in the western region, is technically advanced and moving ahead continuously. Besides, modernization in the engineering industry has been on two levels; low cost automation and high level capital intensive automation.

In the first category, automation is aimed at reducing the fatigue of workers and expediting the tasks of material handling, loading and unloading, etc. For instance, in one engineering company, the loading of steel tubes was done manually. The tube bundles were kept on the fabricated stand and each and every tube was manually pushed by the operator to the machine. After the straightening process by the machine, it was again manually pushed to the unloading bucket by the operator. This system involved a lot of physical effort and the machine capacity was not fully utilized due to time taken for the manual loading and unloading. In the new automated system, the tubes were automatically lifted from the separated bundle and fed into the loading trough. Through its feeding system, the loading trough further automatically pushed the tubes inside the machine. The tubes were straightened and then unloaded into the collecting bucket. This method facilitated straightening of various sizes of tubes and improved efficiency in material handling. Similarly low cost automation was introduced in manufacturing methods through simple pneumatic, hydraulic, electric, mechanical and electronic devices for improving productivity through fatigue reduction.

In the fabrication processes, automation is mainly intro-duced in methods of welding and material handling. Jobs like lifting a number of panels, loading them on to a jig, clamping them into position and arc welding a seam to join them, and then transferring the welded pieces for the next stage of production were done manually. With mechanized cutting and welding, work output increased considerably; work content, delays and rework were reduced and above all, the quality of welding improved tremendously. As an overall impact, this refinement in work processes resulted in the reduction of cycle time of manufacturing the principal end product. This reduction generated additional capacity by savings in man-hours and manufacturing costs.

In the fabrication processes, welding is the crux of job operations. Therefore, innovations and technological upgradations have been focused upon welding. Changes in coil welding, titanium welding, introduction of chemical fabrication and gas-cutting improved the quality of welding and made the process less laborious. Similarly, change in coil winding methods and tube-handling systems also contributed to the ease and accuracy of operatives and increased their safety.

The driving force behind the introduction of low cost automation had been a budget exercise which created an awareness about capacity utilization, control of inputs and material flow. The additional man-hours generated through the cycle time reduction have been utilized in product diversification through the reorganization of manpower. Continuous technological upgradation eliminates the manual skill content in engineering jobs which improves consistency in quality and accuracy of operations.

The higher level of technical change in the engineering industry involves the introduction of CNC machines and flexible manufacturing systems. These provide an infrastructure for product refinement, diversification, enhancement of productivity and reduction of manufacturing costs.

As modernization in the engineering industry was continuous, it did not impose a sudden and heavy financial burden on the company as seen in the case of the steel industry. Hence, decisions about modernization were taken and implemented without any delay.

Here again the public sector cable company stood out with a difference; characterized by sheer indifference and slackness so typical of the bureaucracy. In this company, its principal buyer decided to switch over to jelly-filled cables instead of the paper cables. Hence the company was forced to change the product which required heavy investment in imported machinery. The department of telecommunications (DoT) had directed the company to switch over to jelly-filled cables way back in 1986 itself. But the company requested DoT not to phase out paper cables instantaneously so that its financial position would not be drastically affected. The DoT went along with paper cables till 1989 and gave an ultimatum to the cable company for supplying jelly-filled cables. On receiving this ultimatum, the cable company placed an order for machinery. It took one year to reach a memorandum of understanding with the foreign company and obtain machinery. The machinery arrived in the port of Calcutta but lay there for two years due to lack of funds for customs clearance. The new machinery was finally commissioned in 1994. This delay resulted in losing out to competitors in the private sector and in an escalation of manufacturing costs.

This is again an instance of the way our public sector undertakings usually function. Technological change has to be timely with a strong will to make it successful. With demoralized executives, an undisciplined workforce and a lackadaisical (*chalta hai*) work culture, no sophisticated machinery would reap good results. Delays in the public sector were due to managerial indifference and inefficiency. Similar delays in the private sector were caused due to managerial complacency and lack of competition. Textile units in the private sector were no exception to this.

MODERNIZATION IN THE TEXTILE INDUSTRY

Like steel, the textile industry too, has suffered on account of government policies which have treated mills, powerlooms and handlooms as distinct sectors with different yardsticks of regulations. The policy measures have varied from time to time;

encompassing such aspects as types of cloth to be produced, its price, varied imposition of excise duties to restrain one sector and encourage the other. (The textile policy and its politics has been analyzed excellently by Sanjiv Misra[2] and S. R. B. Lead-beater[3]). The powerloom sector received a very partial treatment. Being in the decentralized sector, they received a number of tax concessions. They could evade the regulations pertaining to wages, working hours and statutory facilities and benefits to be given to workers. Powerlooms could thus produce cloth with a higher profit margin.

It is argued that composite mill owners are responsible for the growth of powerlooms through subcontracting of cloth production. Omkar Goswami[4] states, 'in an attempt to circumvent labour laws and reap the benefits of lower wage costs, powerloom sectors have grown with the active encouragement of mill owners-qua-financiers-qua-traders'. J. R. D. Tata[5] once observed,

> ...the principal reason for deterioration (of the mill sector) has been government policies which banned the expansion of the organized industry in order to protect and promote the decentralized sector comprising the handloom and powerloom sector and imposed on the organized sector heavy excise and other duties and controls from which the decentralised sector was largely exempted. This advantage, coupled with virtual freedom from the obligation to ensure fair wages and other benefits to workers resulted in the powerloom industry becoming a formidable competitor, capturing over 71 per cent of the entire cloth market.

The sickness of the textile industry has been analyzed by many committees appointed by the government and researchers as well. In a nutshell, the overworking of looms in the organized sector during the second world war, the decline in productivity due to overmanning and technological obsolescence, the controlled cloth scheme and other restraining policies of the government and proliferation of the power-loom sector are some of the important reasons stated by them. The textile strike of the early eighties further worsened the situation. In pursuit of the protective policy towards labour, the government took over sixteen composite mills in 1968 by forming the National Textile Corporation (NTC) as a governing body. However, due to faulty policies, inefficient management, lack of funds and indecision regarding closure of mills, the NTC has not been able to revive these mills to date. This researcher visited a couple of non-operational NTC mills in Ahmedabad and Bombay. Their condition was beyond description and revival.

It is noteworthy, however, that the NTC subsidiary in the south (Tamil Nadu and Pondicherry) has been doing well due to its continuous modernization. The mills under this subsidiary are mainly spinning mills producing only yarn. Unlike cloth, yarn has quicker saleability. This subsidiary had even closed the weaving operations in some loss-making mills. The work culture in Coimbatore (where the majority of the NTC mills are situated) also was much better than in Bombay and Ahmedabad. Unions were receptive to change. These mills were unaffected during the Bombay textile strike of 1982–83. All these reasons contributed to the better performance of this NTC subsidiary.

In addition to the those taken over by the government in 1968, around 73 textile mills in the private sector were declared sick by banks in 1977. This number increased further to 123 in 1983 and that under NTC management rose to 125. In the case of other subsidiaries, as obvious from its policy statement of 1985, the government realized that modernization on the one hand and reduction of surplus manpower on the other would help the sick mills revive. In view of this and in pursuit of economic liberalization, the government, in its 1991–92 budget, created a National Renewal Fund. It was a safety net for those employees who were likely to be rendered surplus due to modernization. The working of the National Renewal Fund and the problems involved in its implementation are analyzed in chapter seven.

Some textile mills in the private sector have taken timely measures to upgrade their technology, changed the product-mix and moved into the international market which is not easily amenable to the powerlooms sector. The modernization process in the private sector mills under study differed greatly, depending upon the management vision which decided the priorities in modernizing processes. For instance, in the private sector mill in Bombay, the management decided to modernize its weaving operations first in view of obtaining a refined quality for export. Hence, it replaced its looms by the high speed air jet looms. Soon it realized that the prevailing yarn quality was not suitable for the new looms and the yarn breakage rate was high as a result of which the air jet looms were underutilized. The management, then obtained the open end spinning machines to improve yarn quality. The advantages of open end spinning were multi-dimensional. This process eliminated conventional ring frames, interframes and winding processes. Its requirement of labour force was low. It could accept a cheaper raw material and reduce wastage. Thus the new machinery was capable of giving high productivity at a lower cost.

Opinion regarding the appropriateness of air jet looms was divided. Some senior executives felt that modern machinery increased energy costs and the stores and spares cost. More importantly, they felt that Indian cotton and yarn quality was not suitable for the new machinery. The data on energy costs and yarn quality obtained by this researcher supported this statement. However, the chief executive felt that these were 'teething problems' of modernization and could be mastered over time.

As mentioned earlier, changing the product-mix and diversifying into a variety of products is the main option available to composite mills. This approach indeed proved to be a miracle; a turnaround strategy for a private sector mill in Ahmedabad. After trying different varieties of cloth products, it innovated denim which remained its monopoly till recently.

During this changeover, the management did not discard the conventional manufacturing system. Initially it installed the new equipment in one godown. Making denim is a complex and totally different process. The crux of the operations is the coating of yarn with indigo blue and giving it a faded look. The R & D department developed this technique after a rigorous effort and succeeded in mastering the technology. Denim turned out to be the wonder product which gave a new lease of life to the company.

In some textile mills, including a few NTC mills, modernization was focused on spinning operations, since yarn had a ready market unlike cloth. Hence, these mills had closed weaving operations.

SUMMING UP

Modernization processes in steel, engineering and textile are distinct. But they are all aimed at one and the same objective; of improving quality with reduced costs and making the business profitable. For the eternal truth is that the **Business must Survive**. Towards achieving this end, the industries had to make changes in processes, products and move towards technological upgradation. However, the implementation of the modernization programme was remarkably different in each case across public and private sectors. Public sector management with a remarkable exception of the Greenfield plant, was found complacent, non-committed with a lower level of morale. Such work atmosphere affected quality of decisions in terms of timeliness and reliability. In the private sector, on the other hand, decision-making was quicker. The competitive spirit drove them towards greater commitment and concerted efforts.

Implementation of modernization meant a reorganization of the entire shopfloor activity. It has been analyzed in the next chapter.

REFERENCES

1. Bureau of Industrial Costs and Prices, *Report on Comprehensive Study of Integrated Steel Plants in India and International Cost Competitiveness*, Department of Industries, 1990.
2. **Sanjiv Misra**, *India's Textile Sector: A Policy Analysis*, Sage, 1993.
3. **S. R. B. Leadbeater**, *The Politics of Textiles: The Indian Cotton-Mill Industry and the Legacy of Swadeshi 1900–1985*, Sage, 1993.
4. **Omkar Goswami**, 'Indian Textile Industry, 1970–1984: An Analysis of Demand and Supply' *Economic and Political Weekly*, Vol. XX, No. 38, 21 September 1985.
5. **J. R. D. Tata**, Quoted by Leadbeater, supra 3.

4

New Technology and the
Work Organization

Inherent in technological change is the need to reorganize the workplace and the work activity itself. Reshuffling of manpower then follows naturally so as to suit skill requirements conducive to the process change. Hence reorganization of work varies not only across industries but across different departments within a single organization.

Sometimes the modernization process merely reduces the strength of labour force but not necessarily the skill. For instance, in the weaving operations of textile manufacturing, the basic process of weaving has remained unchanged. It is merely expedited through high speed looms. Similar is the case of the change in some types of welding operations.

When the process change eliminates certain stages of production as in open end spinning or in continuous casting of steel, the requirement of manpower automatically comes down.

Reorganization of work activity is thus effected due to the demands of the new technology. Besides, for making business operations cost-effective, managements introduce industrial engineering methods to reduce manpower requirements and to make optimum utilization of available time, raw materials and human resources. All these are directed at the twin objectives of reducing operating costs and enhancing productivity.

ENHANCEMENT OF LABOUR PRODUCTIVITY

Labour productivity is increased in two ways: (*a*) by introducing a multi-skills concept, and (*b*) by making an operative work on multiple machines.

Multi-skills

An operative is taught an additional skill other than his original trade. This improves utilization of time and energy of the existing manpower on the one hand and thus brings down the requirement for manpower. The skills are clubbed together on the basis of job requirement. For instance, in a fabrication factory, fitters were taught elementary tack welding and thus the requirement for the lower level skilled welders was brought down. These fitters were then designated as fabricators. Such combination of skills naturally varies across industries. In the steel industry, a fitter's job was combined with that of a rigger, and the latter's was combined with the millwright's. In the textile industry, however, this system is not implemented due to the nature of the process itself and the availability of cheap and already recruited surplus manpower. The multi-skills concept acts as a double-edged weapon—it improves labour productivity and reduces manpower requirements.

Working on Multiple Machines

Operatives are made to work on multiple machines which are clubbed together on the basis of coherency of operations. Here, based on their cycle time of operation, the loading and unloading of one machine is done during the automatic cycle of the other machine. During this time, the operative has to move from one machine to another which is not very far from his original machine. In an engineering company in Pune, multi-machine operations were very meticulously synchronized by its industrial engineering department. However, the union challenged this change in the industrial court. It alleged that this system was strenuous and led to absenteeism due to fatigue. However, this contention could not be proved and was turned down by the court. The management showed that these operations were planned very carefully giving due allowances for fatigue. Also, they adhered to the norms laid down by the International Labour Organization. Eventually, the management eased the willingness of acceptance by giving one additional wage increment to operatives working on multiple machines. At the time of this study, 200 such operations were clubbed together.

A high level of automation with an optimum number of operatives promotes productivity. In view of this, in a Greenfield integrated steel company, efforts were made to keep the manpower to the minimum and unlike other public sector plants, overmanning was avoided. One way of doing this is to subcontract many of the jobs required in township and in works. As such, the transport and canteen services were subcontracted; for in many industries these are found to be the potential areas of labour unrest. Thus, this steel plant achieved a dual purpose by resorting to subcontracting work. Time offices, too, were dispensed with. Similarly, schools at the steel city township were run by central educational agencies like Central Schools instead of by the plant management. This arrangement automatically brought down the number of employees on the payroll and reduced the costs of remuneration and statutory benefits and improved the output per employee.

REORGANIZATION OF MANPOWER

Thus, the introduction of new technology involves reshuffling of manpower. The reorganization plan is normally designed by the industrial engineering department. It is a scientific job done by systematically studying the nature of activity and the time taken for its completion. However, some process industries visited by this researcher did not have any such department as the management seemed to think that the industrial engineering function was not required because of product variability on account of changing customer demand. This, however, was incorrect. For the scope of industrial engineering is very wide; which includes designing of work layout, reduction of all kinds of wastages and improving the utilization of all kinds of resources. It was interesting to see in almost all companies how the layout of the shopfloor was changed in order to reduce the unnecessary movement and handling of raw material and avoid the zigzag movement of cranes.

Industrial engineering methods of manpower planning strictly follow the requirements of job operations. While they claim to design an ideal system, production personnel allege them to be oblivious of practical problems arising from skill rigidity and a lackadaisical work culture. And both production and industrial engineering blame the personnel executives for obstructing the reorganization process by giving undue importance to union representatives. Such tussles appeared to be universal. They clearly indicated the lack of coordination and team spirit among the executives of these departments.

Selection of Operatives

That new technology reduces the manpower requirement in all industries is a known fact. However, ways of tackling it vary across companies, depending upon the extent of manpower surplus, the availability of existing skills, the adaptability of operatives and union cooperation.

By and large, new technology in many industries demands technical knowledge, alertness and increased time consciousness from operatives. For instance, in the steel melting shop of the private sector integrated steel factory, when the duplex process with open hearth was in operation it would take eight hours for one heat. The new LD process of oxygen steel making took only about 40 minutes for the same job! The earlier process gave operatives more free time between heats while the new technology demanded ultra time consciousness from them. Preference was therefore given to the young, skilled and enthusiastic operatives while launching a new production activity. Selection of such operatives was done by inviting applications internally.

The selection criteria changed across industries. For instance, in the textile industry when air jet looms were installed, the management had to select tall and young operatives in view of the height of the looms and the increased workload. In those companies where trade union rivalry prevailed, the management had to form a new work group of operatives belonging to one union only. In those organizations, where age and the skill of operatives are immaterial in redeployment, the usual principle followed is 'Last Come, First Go'.

In some engineering industries, a no-retrenchment pact is signed on the advent of technological change. Operatives are also assured protection of their wages and incentives. However, in return, they are liable to be transferred anywhere in the factory and placed even two grades lower than their existing grades. Their grade and wage protection has prevented work stoppages in factories covered in this study. However, such job protection has created a lackadaisical work culture on the shopfloor. Levels of labour productivity and resource utilization have remained low due to this work culture.

Resistance

Despite wage and job protection, operatives in this study had resisted their transfer to other departments. In the steel as well as the textile industry, the absorption of operatives took a number of years. Meanwhile these operatives loitered in the plant without any work. Their presence in the factory was essential for getting idle wages. Hence after registering their attendance, they were free to sleep on the shopfloor or play cards. This invariably is the case with all organizations elsewhere having surplus labour. The number of operatives who refuse to undergo any training and take on a job suitable to them are not small. In public sector organizations their resistance is more due to over security of their jobs. Under the existing provisions of the Industrial Disputes Act (chapter V B), lay-off and retrenchment of employees and closure of unviable units employing a minimum of hundred employees is not permissible without prior approval of the government. As this permission is not given on account of a pro-labour policy, companies have evolved a number of ways to achieve their objectives: (*a*) stoppage of fresh recruitment, (*b*) the introduction of multi-skills and a one man crew system, and (*c*) introduction of a voluntary retirement scheme.

In most of the larger companies in the organized sector, recruitment of operatives has been stopped for over a decade. Manual skills are increasingly taken over by machines. Besides as wage levels in engineering industries are high, managements wish to maintain an optimum level of labour force. It helps in curtailing labour costs and their long-term financial liabilities and also, as discussed earlier, limits potential disturbances. The textile industry provides comparatively lower wage levels but the production process is labour intensive and there has been overmanning from the very beginning. As the composite textile mills started facing stiff competition from the powerloom sector, they too started cutting down their labour costs. Many of the companies have now stopped recruitment of sons of the soil and of their own employees.

Removal of a Helper's Category

One way of reducing manpower is by removing the category of helpers altogether. A helper is required to clean the machine and its surroundings, bring tools from the tools stand, get raw material and do all sundry jobs. Companies now want to change this to a one man crew system. Aimed at curtailing labour costs, an operative in this system will have to manage the work activity without a helper's assistance. Operatives everywhere have been resenting this change on the pretext of a heavy workload. The fact, however, is that operatives get an ego-satisfaction of bossing over a helper. In the steel industry, at times, operatives were found to be 'bribing' the helpers with a lunch coupon for doing their strenuous jobs. They would even take a nap after 'delegating' their job to the helpers.

In the public sector steel plant, the helper's category seemed to have provided the opportunity to fulfil its objective of generating employment. As such there were helpers attached to each skilled and semi-skilled categories of operatives. Thus, there were fitter-helpers, welder-helpers, rigger-helpers at the ratio of one helper per skilled operative. The management has now tried to change this system and ensure job flexibility by introducing a cluster concept through an agreement with the union.

The Cluster Concept

Under this arrangement, various grades and skills were combined into three categories, namely, cluster A, B and C. For instance, in the blast furnace of the public sector integrated steel company grades L-1 and L-2 were clubbed together to form cluster A and given the designation of junior technician. Cluster B comprised grades L-3 to L-7 and all the operatives in this cluster were categorized as technicians. Operatives in the upper grades of L-8 and L-9 were designated chargemen in cluster C. The purpose of bringing the chargemen under one cluster was to eliminate the compartmentalization of maintenance activity and prevent the obstruction in the smooth flow of production. The cluster system was thus aimed at wiping out the divisions and subdivisions of tasks. It was also aimed at facilitating the horizontal and vertical movement of operatives across hierarchical categories. It was expected to improve manpower utilization with a simultaneous check on the malpractices of operatives claiming acting allowance by mutual convenience. In order to reduce grade stagnation among operatives, it was decided to promote them within the same cluster after completion of five years. Promotion from one cluster to the next would be subject to the fulfilment of minimum qualifications, other parameters of eligibility and the passing of trade tests.

As this cluster concept appeared to be the best solution to remove skill rigidity and reduce interruptions in workflow it had been introduced at the Greenfield steel plant. The bargainable category of employees comprised only three grades, namely, unskilled (L-1 and L-2 grades), skilled technicians (L-3, L-4 and L-5 grades) and chargemen (L-6, L-7 grades). At the level of technicians and chargemen, the concept of multi-skilling was introduced. However, the line managers stated that a work culture conducive to work flexibility was lacking, as a result of which officers were overburdened with jobs.

GROUP DYNAMICS ON THE SHOPFLOOR

Reorganization of shopfloor activity affects group relations among operatives. They are reluctant to leave their work group and move to another in some other department. As mentioned earlier, in those organizations where more than one union and faction groups exist, the management takes care to place together only those operatives belonging to one union. However, government rulings, unmindful of such realities, have disturbed industrial relations. This was observed in a textile mill in Ahmedabad and also in a steel factory in Bombay.

The case of the steel factory in Bombay provides an interesting example. There the management sought permission from the government to set up a technically advanced rolling bar mill near Bombay. The permission was granted with two preconditions. The first required the management to dismantle the old rolling mill within six months of the first trial run of the bar mill at the new location. The second precondition laid down that nearly 140 operatives from the old mill should be absorbed in three phases at the new rolling mill.

In observance of this ruling, when the management issued transfer orders to 50 operatives at the old location, the union resisted their transfers by declaring a sit-down strike. The management then filed a suit against the union alleging an unfair labour practice of an illegal strike.

The industrial court, while upholding the management's action, turned down the union's contention that the transfer orders were malafide. It observed that the company had merely obeyed the condition laid down by the government. The court also dismissed the union's argument that the operatives would be prejudicially affected because of the difference in the work process and the respective job evaluation at both the places. The court observed that the job evaluation is an eventual task to be undertaken only after the mill starts functioning. When the operatives work at the bar mill for some time, their jobs could be evaluated.

The union further argued that there was a basic difference in the working conditions at the old and the new plant and by an agreement between the management and the union at the new location, operatives were required to switch over from one trade to another by undergoing training. This, the union contended, would put the operatives at a great disadvantage. The industrial court, however, dismissed this plea too. It laid down that 'the company has a right to effect transfer and if the transfer is for administrative and business exigencies, the worker is bound to obey the order of transfer. Again, he cannot make any grievance as regards some minor differences in the terms of settlements applicable to the two units of the same company'.

Thus the court upheld the cause of business exigency and the company's adherence to the government's preconditions while allowing dismantling of the old mill. The operatives were transferred from the old mill to the new mill.

The workers, however, could not adjust themselves to the new work environment. The work culture and level of discipline were different at the new workplace. Educationally, too, they were behind their counterparts at the new location. They found it difficult to adjust to the changed workgroup. Due to the combined effect of all these, clashes between the two groups were not uncommon and the supervisors had a tough time settling disputes and achieving production targets. They would then ignore the idle and reluctant operatives and get the work done from the sincere and conscientious operatives. This at times demoralized the good employees.

The point to be driven home is that while the issue of new technology is not disputed by the union, its support to workers' adamance for redeployment is the biggest bottleneck in the smooth operation of new technology across all industries and regions in India. Internal deployment of operatives is essential for improving labour productivity and making new technology a success. Realizing this, the unions should change their adamant stand. Redeployment should not be made an issue in industrial relations.

However, as the unions have resisted shopfloor reorganization, the engineering companies in the private sector in the western region have made counter-demands in wage settlements that internal redeployment is a managerial prerogative and that the operatives are required to follow the changed work system. The managements have preserved their rights to effect technological change, introduce new work methods, set work norms and quality standards. These prerogatives have been continuously and explicitly reiterated in the three-yearly wage settlements. This practice has been prevailing in the western region since the beginning of the eighties. As a result of this, matters pertaining to work reorganization associated with technological change have been kept out of union interference. This trend is now slowly moving to other industries and regions. In a private sector textile mill in Ahmedabad, workers resisted redeployment and sat idle for nearly two years. The union representative at this mill admitted that the provision in the earlier settlement stating that operatives would move to *other departments of their own choice* had proved to be a mistake. For, despite the noble objective of giving workers a choice, they were not adaptive. Hence, in the three-yearly wage settlement, the management changed this clause. According to the changed clause, it was imperative for the operatives to move to the *departments of the management's choice.*

SPADEWORK WITH COORDINATION

Reorganization of shopfloor activity requires considerable spadework by the departments of industrial engineering, production and personnel. This spadework should commence the moment the policy decision regarding introduction of new technology is taken by the management. The industrial engineering and production divisions have to design the new work layout, decide on norms of output and the required skills and the strength of the employees. The HRD has to implement the reorganization plan.

Shopfloor organization is a crucial task not free from potential industrial unrest. The prime responsibility of the management is to create an atmosphere conducive to training and the acceptance of change. The next chapter presents various aspects of training essential for a smooth implementation of new technology.

5

Training: The Indispensable Spadework

To set in motion the process of modernization a coordinated effort of training employees is needed. There are no shortcuts to this activity; it should commence well in advance, prior to the arrival of new machinery.

By and large, training gained importance only since the late eighties, when the business organizations in India had to shed complacency and face competition. The compelling need to obtain an ISO-9000 certificate has led managements to give special attention to the training activity. Under the guidelines for obtaining this certificate, there is a special schedule (schedule 4.17 of ISO-9002 for instance) emphasizing 'identification of training needs, organization of appropriate training programmes either in-house or by an outside body and recording of training and achievement in order to identify gaps in training and update the programmes'. Most of the companies covered in this study seemed to have realized this compelling need for training. The only exceptions to these were the public sector integrated steel company and an engineering company in the private sector. Training had been totally ignored in the textile industry. Workers normally joined as 'substitutes' to permanent employees for a temporary period and learnt their jobs from a jobber or other colleagues in the department.

Under such circumstances and the prevailing business culture, training was viewed as an unnecessary expenditure and the entire effort was focused merely upon production. Although training is a neutral activity, supposedly free from union influence, the fact remains that it can take place only in a cordial atmosphere, free from tensions of strained relations between management and union. As such, among the companies examined in this study only those with a good record of industrial peace instituted systematic training programmes which extended to the grassroot level operatives. In other cases, training was confined only to the management trainees and middle and top level executives who were sent to prestigious institutes which in their view was a 'paid holiday'.

With an increasing awareness about creating goodwill among employees and equipping them with skills demanded by new technology, training activity in business organizations now has received a new outlook and a different approach.

TRAINING AND TECHNOLOGICAL CHANGE

Like all facets of work organization or ensuing modernization, training activity too has to be devised in consultation with industrial engineering and production executives. The personnel department is involved in the most basic tasks without which no plan of modernization can be made operational. These are (*a*) sharing of information; (*b*) preparing employees mentally to accept change; and (*c*) training them in new skills and job operations.

In actuality, the first two stages are not separable. They should be launched as a finely mingled information-sharing drive. Such an approach is indicative of expressing confidence in employees. Decisions pertaining to the proposed purchase of new technology should be communicated soon after the memorandum of understanding is signed between the employer and the collaborator. Any such event poses the most basic threat of the possible skill redundancy and of being surplus and hence unwanted in the organization. In order to allay these apprehensions, the management is required to do a good deal of homework. They have to work out the details regarding the man–machine ratio, capacity utilization, input of raw materials, requirement of energy and input from other departments.

Concomitant with this exercise is the task of maintaining good work morale by removing uncertainty about one's job requirement due to the forthcoming technological change. This has to be done by educating employees through formal and informal channels. Formal channels comprise notice boards and meetings with union representatives. Informal channels of such education can be limited only by imagination. Daily interactions with supervisors, weekly meetings with departmental managers, putting up posters, organizing film shows and establishing communication through in-house journals are some of them.

The most important message to be put across through these meetings is the importance of new technology, its advantages and indispensability.

Simple though it appears, information-sharing is the most neglected aspect of employee involvement in the process of modernization. In some companies, the proposed technological change was an 'information shock' through the statutory notice of change and the arrival of the new machinery. They suddenly found themselves to be surplus and hence without any work. In one private sector textile mill, even the middle cadre employees, who were eventually required to put the new machinery into operation were denied access to its technical information and manuals. Under the circumstances, how could the management expect their cooperation?

It is essential that prior to the actual commencement of training on new machines these misconceptions are removed. This is the first and foremost stage of preparing employees mentally to accept change. This preparation starts with removing misconceptions of workers that the new work process would be complex and laborious. In the textile industry, for instance, managers mentioned that it took a lot of time and patience to allay the workers' misconception that the new work process would be complex and laborious. As seen in the previous chapter, new technology requires skill flexibility. Hence, even prior to imparting training in new skills, creating a favourable atmosphere for skill flexibility should be the prime objective of the training activity.

Skill flexibility and adaptability to change are dependent upon the overall educational level of employees. For instance, adaptability levels were much lower in steel and textile industries in comparison with the engineering industry. Managers in the textile industry mentioned that it took much time and effort to convey to the workers that working on air jet looms did not necessarily mean a highly complicated job. On the other hand, workers in the engineering industry took pride in being selected to work on the CNC machine. Similar was the case of those welders who were selected for training in titanium welding. Such selection was viewed as an indicator of their efficiency and intelligence.

Training activity can be broadly classified into three categories. (*a*) Training in the training school run by the organization itself. (*b*) On the job training by engaging external experts often sent by the technical collaborators. (*c*) Sending employees to other technical institutes within the country or even outside in exceptional cases.

SELECTION OF EMPLOYEES FOR TRAINING

As training involves expenditure, the natural tendency of the management is to select young employees. The other criteria are determined by the demands of the new technology itself. For instance, the height of the air jet looms was more than the old Ruti looms. Hence only tall employees could be selected to work on the latter. Elsewhere, in the south when management could not consider height as one of the criteria (due to the small frame of people in the region) workers had to be provided with wooden stools. The management had also ignored the 'pot bellies' of these workers. (Funny perhaps as it would appear but the pot bellies indeed posed a problem in workers' movements around the looms.) Working on the air jet looms meant a higher incentive due to increased productivity. Hence the selected operatives had to be efficient and have a good service record. They had to 'deserve' the investment in them as well as the increased earnings. While selecting employees for imparting training in specific skills, the most important criteria were their trade and level of efficiency. But this was not so when selecting candidates for training programmes on non-technical subjects, varying from health and hygiene to company information.

The non-technical and technical training programmes were viewed as a pleasant diversion from the daily routine. Hence, supervisors recommended the names of those workers who had stood by them by working hard. Thus some people were sent for training more frequently while some did not get a single chance. It was not surprising, therefore, that workers perceived management as 'partial and unfair'.

Training was often viewed as a leisure time activity. Production personnel were stated to be reluctant to relieve operatives for training for fear of losing production. But in times of a demand slump due to recession, they kept the workers engaged in some training programme or the other.

Ideally, training should be a neutral activity; free from trade union interference and politics. Trade unions should be involved by way of positive consultation but matters pertaining to training should never be negotiated. Normally, however, it is not so because training is linked to either promotion or wage increment. In one integrated steel company, where the management was too lenient and feared the union, the latter forced the management to pass the entire batch of operatives who had failed in a trade test conducted by the training department.

Some companies even trained a few workers abroad. Such training was a part of the package of technology transfer from the collaborator. Those trained abroad were then asked to train their colleagues back home. Exposure to training abroad did help in improving their awareness about work culture and loyalty towards the organization. However, such work consciousness remained only at the personal level. The workers could not disseminate it as was the management's natural expectation from them.

As mentioned earlier, training has been a long neglected area in the textile industry and in the public sector in general. Only the compulsion of market competition led these companies into self-retrospection. It revealed that the reason for yarn breakages was more due to wrong methods of piecing the sliver. Similarly the method of lifting the sliver, too, was found defective. These methods were set right when the company set up a 100 per cent Export-Oriented Unit.

In yet another textile mill which was on the verge of being taken over by the Board for Industrial and Financial Reconstructing (BIFR), management decided to invest in training rather than in buying new machinery. With a view to improving the work culture, the management devised two types of training courses. (*a*) Freshers' Training Programme and (*b*) Refresher Training Programme. The duration of the first training programme was three weeks involving one hour theory and seven hours' practical work. Good workers and three officers were nominated as instructors. They clearly observed the trainee workers who were selected in batches of ten to fifteen. Samples of their work were taken randomly and analyzed. In the case of low efficiency and defective work, reasons were explored and explained to the trainees. They were taught machine drawings and other technical aspects of work. As part of this programme, a maintenance audit was created. Machines were required to be maintained regularly and workers were taught to maintain them.

After 21 days of training, tests were conducted and workers' efficiency was assessed. Performance was rewarded and recognized. But failure was not viewed negatively. The training schedule was planned in such a manner that every worker received training at least once a year. Details of refresher training were being worked out at the time of this fieldwork.

This training activity contributed tremendously towards creating quality consciousness and also helped workers develop positive work behaviour. On the whole it helped develop a positive attitude towards the company.

A most notable example in devising training programmes to suit the requirements of skill flexibility of workers was that of an engineering company in Pune. Its management had formulated a unique scheme of linking a wage increment to learning an additional skill so as to keep the workers motivated by providing them growth opportunities.

Wage increments were linked to obtaining a higher level skill (*a*) in the original trade of an operative, (*b*) in the trades of the original department and (*c*) in some few trades which were clubbed together in view of utility. These were known as cross versatility benefits encompassing the departments of production, maintenance and inspection.

A number of preconditions were laid down as eligibility criteria for appearing for the benefit tests. These were:

1. The candidate should have completed a minimum of two years of service after passing of a test of either skill or versatility benefit.
2. He should not have been given a suspension or warning for any misconduct during the two years' qualifying period mentioned.
3. The candidate should not have been absent unauthorizedly for more than three days during the entire year prior to applying for the said benefit.

Accompanying the application for the trade test, the candidate was required to enclose his supervisor's evaluation report of his job. This evaluation pertained to the operative's rate of output, dependability of quality, self-inspection, housekeeping and cooperation with the supervisor. The break-up of evaluation weightages was as follows:

30 per cent for departmental evaluation
20 per cent for interview
50 per cent for trade test
(40 per cent for job accuracy and 10 per cent for adherence to its time limit and speed)

The noteworthy feature of this scheme was that operatives did not get a vacancy-based promotion from one grade to another. Their upgradation was subject to the passing of a trade test. Growth opportunities for operatives were very few; besides, their manual skills were increasingly taken over by a machine. In such a situation, this scheme combined learning and financial gains. Above all, it had helped the management in creating a flexible workforce. Once an operative obtained a monetary benefit under the scheme, both legally and morally he could not refuse a job on being deployed to another department.

Although ideally designed, this scheme was not free from problems arising out of functional distortion. During interviews with this researcher, some supervisors admitted that the skill benefit was given as a reward to those loyal and hard-working operatives who stood by them in times of need. The passing of the test was easy because of the 30 per cent weightage given to supervisory assessment. The trade tests were not taken very seriously till the recent past as both supervisors and operatives assumed that the new skill obtained was unlikely to be utilized. Besides, the supervisors were hesitant in transferring operatives to jobs other than their original trades in order to keep the production quota unaffected.

These functional distortions became more evident when the operatives were redeployed on a huge scale due to the changes in the production requirements accruing from the market demands. The market situations demanded a shift in the focus of production activity from one product to another. In the internal reshuffling of the operatives, it soon became obvious that those deployed were the unwanted or mediocre operatives. Simultaneously, being aware that their deployment was temporary, the deployed operatives did not take their jobs very seriously. Their supervisors had to train them because they could not perform the job efficiently despite having passed the trade test earlier. This was because the operatives' skills had gone rusty due to non-utilization.

Another major lacuna concerned the level of skill obtained through this scheme. Most of the operatives had obtained versatility benefit at the lower level of their respective grades. For instance, most of the fitters of operative grade had obtained versatility of the same grade and the same level of another trade, such as the welder's. This level of skill (i.e., of their original level) could not always ensure the required quality of output on being redeployed.

Despite such lacunae, the skill versatility benefit scheme does have a number of advantages. The biggest among them is the non-disruption of operations even in the event of absenteeism or reduced work activity in some departments due to lack of orders.

The aforementioned defects in the system can easily be removed by introducing a job rotation system on a regular basis. It will serve the dual purpose of gaining maximum benefits of training and remove job-monotony of operatives. Concomitantly, it is also essential that the operatives are encouraged to obtain versatility skills at higher levels. If the operatives are equipped with higher level multi-skills and constantly practise them through rotation, redeployment would fetch better results. It would also curtail trade imbalance which is not uncommon in industry.

By and large, business organizations are now increasingly recognizing the value of training. This was observed particularly in two Greenfield organizations; in the 100 per cent export unit of an engineering company in the private sector and an integrated steel company in the public sector.

When the 100 per cent Export-Oriented Unit (EOU) was about to be set up, children of 60 per cent of the employees in the parent organization were selected through an aptitude test. The management preferred to take those who had finished only schooling and train them rather than recruit those who had studied in technical institutes. The managers mentioned that they were not very happy about the training imparted in these institutes. Besides they wished to avoid 'technical branding' of operatives as welders and fitters, which usually was the case of the products of the technical institutes. The management wanted a flexible workforce to suit the special skill requirements of its highly automated EOU. It, therefore, approached a. well-known welding research institute in south India. The management's novel idea of devising a multi-skill training course was new even to this training institute and hence it was not accepted readily. With great perseverance on the part of the management, the course was finally designed and training was imparted to fresh recruits in the areas of welding, wheel assembly and painting. Thorough training was imparted in safety and self-inspection of quality of output. Workers were trained even in the cleaning of machines and housekeeping. By and large workers were trained to be self-sufficient in a variety of job operations.

In the public sector integrated steel plant too, training activity was aimed at creating a workforce of multi-disciplinary skills. During training, they were taught dignity of labour through assignments of various jobs. They were given training in special as well as general skills; especially skills pertaining to particular trades. The lack of common skills has often proved an obstruction in the smooth flow of work. Some of these common skills were related to an elementary knowledge about electricity, fuses, switches and voltmeters. Training was also aimed at developing the ability to detect faults in mechanical equipment and lubricating the same.

After this basic training, workers were sent to integrated steel plants in other parts of the country. They were required to be trained in operating steel melt shops and mills which were still to be commissioned.

Training is a continuous activity. But even in this plant, it was difficult to maintain the tempo due to heavy absenteeism which prevented production managers from releasing workers for training.

THE LACUNAE

The crux of training lies in identifying training needs prior to designing the programme. This should be done in consultation with heads of departments. By and large, such coordination between the training and other departments was rare. Though the training programmes were designed to facilitate skill flexibility, the operatives were not given an opportunity to practise the same. The prime responsibility of making full use of these skills lay with the shopfloor managers. But they were hesitant due to the potential decrease in production and sub-standard quality.

There has to be a continuous feedback on training programmes by those who engage trainees to work on the shopfloor. This type of coordination too did not exist in many organizations covered in this study.

TRAINING THE MIDDLE CADRE EMPLOYEES

Studies in industrial sociology have shown that middle cadre employees everywhere are an ignored class. This author had highlighted their problems in her earlier publication (see chapter 2, note 9). In the present study, too, management seemed to have focused their training activity on the workers and neglected training at the supervisory level. The importance of training for any person in any cadre cannot be over-emphasized. Providing an opportunity to learn something new is one important means of maintaining employee morale.

Just as skill flexibility is absolutely essential for operatives, middle cadre employees should be aware of and attentive to the interconnections of their primary job responsibility with other departments. For instance, a production supervisor should know about costing and marketing of his departmental output. This will increase his cost and quality consciousness. It is noteworthy that such an exposure was given in only one engineering organization in south India. The job demarcations there were blurred due to a change in the organizational set-up and better communication with supervisors. Supervisors were involved in inter-departmental meetings. This improved their awareness about the performance of their own department and of the entire organization. They were also sent for training in job-related areas.

Training is a part of organizational culture. It should be built up with a spirit of teamwork and employee participation. It should be linked to performance appraisal by giving due consideration to individual choice and aptitude.

Hence, desirable though it may be, training, in many organizations, is not a totally neutral activity independent of trade union interference and politics. In such cases managements will have to make conscious efforts to stop this interference. The process of introducing new technology cannot be successful without trade union cooperation. In fact, the trade union–management relationship pervasively gives a nuance to every aspect of organizational activity. The next chapter has been focused on the union–management dynamics influencing the transition from the old technology to the new.

6

Modernization and
Union–Management Dynamics

Traditionally and universally, unions are believed to be opposed to automation due to its job displacing effect. Over time, however, they have moved towards its acceptance through negotiations over the 'price of change'.

Decisions pertaining to purchase of new technology have essentially been a managerial prerogative; an outcome of the financial stakes. Employees and their unions cannot question the choice of technology. They are merely involved in redeployment of employees, their gradations and wage increments.

Union resistance to voluntary retirement schemes also has traversed from outright rejection to bargained acceptance. The intensity of union approaches has varied across regions, industries and sectors. It has a bearing upon the strength of the union and the financial condition of the company, educational level of the employees and the overall industrial relations atmosphere in the region.

In the context of technological change, union involvement occurs essentially in two aspects, namely (*a*) re-organization of the work activity and (*b*) implementation of the voluntary retirement scheme. Out of these, the second aspect is discussed separately in chapter eight.

TRADE UNION INVOLVEMENT IN THE WORK REORGANIZATION

We have seen in chapter four how the advent of new technology generates manpower surplus which requires redeployment through training. Unions have now come to accept this process as an inevitable fact of working life. However, they bargain for higher wage increments and incentives commensurate with the increased productivity due to automation. Their approaches, as mentioned earlier, vary across industries, regions and sectors. These are now analyzed.

Steel

Industry and region are the major determinants of the personnel practices and the overall climate of industrial relations. In a country like India, these factors are more decisive because of tremendous diversity in geographical, socio-economic, and cultural factors in different regions. For instance, most of the integrated steel factories in both private and public sectors are situated in Bihar, Madhya Pradesh and West Bengal. Though endowed with abundant mineral deposits and natural resources essential for making steel, the states of Bihar and Madhya Pradesh have remained socially and economically backward. A few criteria used for assessing the backwardness of states are (*a*) life expectancy at birth; (*b*) infant mortality rate; (*c*) literacy rate; (*d*) per capita income; and (*e*) extent of urbanization. Being a relative term, backwardness has to be assessed in comparison with other states or all India averages. From this point of view, data presented in Table 6.1 highlight the

TABLE 6.1

Assessment of Backwardness in a Few States

States	Life expectancy at birth (years) 1986–90	Infant mortality rate, 1993	Literacy rate (%)	Per capita income (Rs) 1992–93 (provisional)	Extent of Urbanization
					Percentage of urban population to total population
Punjab	65.2	55	58.5	10,857	29.55
Haryana	62.2	65	55.8	9,609	24.84
Maharashtra	62.6	50	64.9	9,270	38.65
Gujarat	57.7	58	61.3	7,586	34.38
Karnataka	61.1	67	56.0	6,313	30.88
West Bengal	60.8	58	57.7	5,901	27.44
Kerala	69.5	13	89.8	5,065	26.46
Madhya Pradesh	53.0	106	44.2	4,725	23.14
Bihar	54.9	70	38.5	3,280	13.19
All India	57.7	74	52.2	6,234	25.71

Source: Economic Survey 1994–95; Statistical Outline 1995–96.
Note: Infant mortality rate is the number of infants dying under one year of age in a year per 1,000 live births in the same year.

backwardness of states where most of the integrated steel companies are situated.

Thus these companies have had to depend upon unskilled and illiterate local labour and induct technically qualified employees from other states. The extreme climatic conditions and hazardous nature of work add to the management's difficulties in handling personnel problems. Besides, the slightest disruption in the continuous process of making steel amounts to heavy short-term and long-term losses. The managements in steel industry everywhere, therefore, seem to have adopted a benevolent and soft approach to attract and retain employees. In the private sector company, many of the welfare measures were initiated even before they were made obligatory statutorily. Similarly, in the public sector company covered in this study the employer's approach of concern, care and integrated community development was reflected in the facilities provided at the township.

The soft approaches of managements in integrated steel companies led them to ignore workers' tendency to loiter, sleep on the shopfloor and by and large follow a leisurely routine at work. The unions took full advantage of the management's leniency and exercised their 'power' to control the process flow. The chain action process of making steel promoted their power. Owing to this process, if production in one department was disrupted, it automatically brought the entire plant on the verge of a standstill. This fear compelled the management to be extra liberal in terms of tolerating undue interference of unions. As an example, in one company it was agreed upon by both the union and the management in their memorandum of settlement that technological change was a managerial prerogative. A clause to this effect in the settlement stated explicitly that the union recognized the right of the company to eliminate, change or consolidate jobs, sections, departments or divisions; provided that when the employees' interests were likely to be adversely affected, the union was to be consulted before the management took a decision. As per this clause, the union was required to be consulted only when the change was detrimental to workers' interests. In practice, however, the union insisted that no change was implemented without their consent. The union kept these proposals pending for a long time, often exceeding a year. Whenever vacancies arose during the process of labour rationalization, the union insisted on filling up the vacancies by promoting the workers down the line. It then raised the issue of their reclassification on account of increased workload. At times workers were upgraded and yet the contract labour was engaged to get the same job done. Cases of reclassification of grades were decided by the Permanent Joint Rates Committee comprising a high level managerial team and union officials. In pursuance of their short-sighted ways of bringing industrial peace, the managers took a liberal approach and conceded to the union's demands of upgradation. They failed to visualize the plantwide repercussions of their decision and its financial burden to the company. Once a set of workers were given higher grades, the very same union officials would bring another group of workers in the same category from other departments and place a demand for their upgradation.

With the very same militant spirit the union pressurized the management to change a clause relating to sickness benefit. Accordingly, the clause providing for sickness benefit for those injured on works (i.e., within factory premises) changed to injured on duty. It thereby increased the scope for misuse and manoeuvring of injuries on duty (which encompassed even a slightest scratch on the body incurred on the way to the factory).

The middle cadre employees responsible for production and production-related shopfloor activities were highly demoralized due to such soft approaches of the senior management.

Whether a steel plant had one single and strong union or a multiplicity of unions, their nuisance value did not vary in intensity due to the very nature of the work process. The Greenfield steel plant, too, was not an exception. Here an overwhelming majority of workers belonged to the first generation of industrial workers. As such they lacked maturity in their interactions with management. They failed to internalize the implications of negotiations with the management and the binding effect of a settlement. Hence the managers stated that even if the leaders agreed to follow a certain practice, there was no guarantee that the workers would accept their leaders' decisions. However, the union could not interfere with areas earmarked as managerial prerogatives; of intra-plant transfers, disciplinary actions and promotions.

The steel factory in Bombay was prominent in so far as the union–management interaction was concerned. After the failure of the long drawn-out textile strike in Bombay, the workers in other industries too became aware of the futility of striking over unjustified and unreasonable demands. The managements from other industries gave up their soft approaches towards organized labour. A new trend of placing counter-demands on unions during wage negotiations set in. The leader of the textile strike in Bombay also happened to be the leader of the workers' union at the steel factory. His failure in the textile strike made the management adopt a very tough stand during the 13 months closure of the plant. They brought skilled workers from all over India to run the factory. These workers were given accommodation on the factory premises. They were brought in with an understanding that their services would be terminated once the lockout ended. When the striking workers of the steel factory saw that the management could do away with them and that they were not indispensable, they gave up their struggle and accepted virtually all the conditions laid down by the management in the bilateral settlement. However, as a precautionary measure the management avoided the operation of the ultra high power furnace by workers for fear of sabotage. It was run by supervisors for quite some time.

The trend of adopting a tough stand against worker militancy and placing counter-demands in wage settlements is widely prevalent in the engineering industry in western India. We shall presently move on to this phenomenon.

Engineering Industry

Unlike the steel industry, in the engineering industry, change on the shopfloor due to reorganization of work has been a well-guarded managerial prerogative. It was noteworthy that the managements had preserved their prerogative in respect to setting up time standards, recruitment, selection, promotion and deployment of operatives. They had also preserved their right to effect technological change, introduce new work methods and set up production and quality standards. These prerogatives continued to be reiterated in wage settlements since the early eighties. Consequently, matters related to technological change were kept out of union interference. But more importantly, technological change was smooth due to a higher educational level of workers in the engineering industry as against those in steel and textile industries overmanned by illiterate operatives. Nearly all the skilled operatives in the engineering industry in the western region were technically qualified. The minimum essential qualification for direct recruits was SSC (with 60 per cent marks) and a technical diploma from Industrial Training Institutes or a NCVT (National Council for Vocational Trade) certificate. One engineering company also had a system of absorbing full-time apprentices after they underwent a rigorous residential training course for three years. Besides a greater emphasis on in-house training had been laid from the very inception of the factory. As a combined effect of all these factors, the operatives and unions in this industry were quite aware of the necessity to move with the times by continuous upgradation of technology.

Job security and economic prosperity are important determinants of operatives' acceptance of new technology. Most of the managements (including those in this study) of the engineering industry in the western region have entered into no-retrenchment agreements on account of technological change. They could do it because unlike the steel and textile industries, their organizations were never overmanned. They had maintained an optimum level of manpower from the very beginning. Also, their organizations were of fairly recent origin spanning about 25 to 30 years. This meant that their technology too was less labour-intensive when compared with that in textile and steel. High labour cost in the western region was another compelling factor for being cautious about manpower planning. Here whenever automation was introduced, manpower redundancy was not huge. Besides as these operatives were technically qualified, they could be absorbed elsewhere due to their better technical adaptability.

Yet redeployment and introduction of skill flexibility were not uniformly smooth. In one fabrication process oriented company, the closure of a machine shop rendered 120 operatives surplus. They were laid off with full pay for about nineteen months while an application for their retrenchment was made to the Commissioner of Labour. The union naturally resisted this move and counter-demanded the retrenchment of technical staff and other middle cadre employees. About one-third of those who were laid off left the company. While the retrenchment application was still pending with the Commissioner, there was a change in the management team. The new executives decided to absorb the surplus workers subject to their willingness for retraining at the company's expense at the Vocational Training School. Those absorbed were given one higher grade and two wage increments. While this agreement helped patch up differences between union and management, it also created a bad precedent for frequent interferences of the union in job gradations. Whenever a new activity came up and the workers were required to be redeployed there, the union took the opportunity to demand a revision of grades. By allowing such interferences, the management could not guard its discretion (though agreed upon by the union) 'to deploy any workman to do any work in a category/trade other than the existing trade of the workman'. The provision that the deployment period would not exceed six months was another potential area of union–management differences.

Through this agreement multi-skilling was introduced by giving an additional allowance of Rs 4 per day for those who were asked to do an additional job other than that in their specified trade. The operatives were reluctant to do such additional jobs due to this negligible amount. Some of the trades like grinder/polishing were considered of inferior status. Besides they also feared loss of overtime and incentive payment in their original departments. The union had no control over such employees who refused to be redeployed. By entering into agreements with a specific group of employees it had also created a subtle rift among its own members. The difference in facilities further intensified this rift. For instance, except for fitters, the other operatives were given free milk and biscuits. Such partiality hampered the team spirit of employees. The managerial personnel, therefore, had a tough time in fulfilling their production targets.

These managers tackled such work-related problems through increased subcontracting of jobs and payment of overtime wages. Nearly 58 per cent of the total production was off-loaded. That the practice of giving overtime wages is very unhealthy and susceptible to manoeuvring is quite well known. The available statistics showed that the value of production per available man-hour was less than the overtime wage per man-hour. Hence it was not justified. Yet the management seemed to overlook this fact for fear of turbulent industrial relations and potential losses. The trade union executives privately admitted that their members had become 'addicted' to overtime wage earnings. They, however, were unable to check this unhealthy trend.

Southern Region

Union–management dynamics were different in the engineering companies of the southern region. In many organizations, the management virtually controlled the unions and 'boasted' of industrial peace. Such 'benevolent dictatorship' worked when the company's financial condition was good. However, in times of recession, as observed in the case of one company, there was a jolt to cohesion resulting in an outburst of unrest. The trade unions drew support on the basis of castes rather than on their activities.

In the public sector engineering organization covered in this study, over security of jobs and complacency of the management had contributed to the union's adamance towards skill rigidity and resistance to redeployment of operatives. The union was totally unconcerned with unproductive work practices, many of which are detailed in the next chapter.

Textile

As stated earlier in chapter three, the production of textile is a labour-intensive process. Till the textile strike in Bombay in

1982–83, the Bombay mills functioned in a complacent atmosphere.[1] Surplus manpower was one of the reasons for low productivity. After the strike manpower was substantially and consciously reduced through modernization. While the modernization process was in full swing, the rival and unrecognized unions which were responsible for the 1982 strike, tried to stage a comeback. They instigated a few workers to oppose the removal of dismantled old looms and the installation of new machinery. Some dismissed employees and those likely to be displaced due to modernization were easily swayed by the leader's provocations. This event clearly indicated how trade union politics played an obstructing role in the process of implementing technological change. The extent of union resistance was more in the public sector. In some cases, they even opposed the changing of the shop layout. They always took legal recourse to resist work-related change which meant further delay and losses of opportunity costs of modernization. Workers in the textile industry were easily swayed by the provocations of leaders mainly because of their low level of education, mostly varying between fourth to ninth standard.

Yet the worker–union relationship was independent of the management–worker relationship and the union–management relationship. These three levels of interactions existed on different planes. These are now analyzed.

Union–Worker Relationship

For an ordinary, uneducated union member, a union representative is the entire union itself. A department level union representative is an image builder of the union. He, therefore, has a lot of responsibility in communicating union approaches, helping a member solve his work-related problems and function as a lynchpin of the union. As observed and confirmed through discussions with operatives and the senior union office bearers, many of the department level union representatives in textile mills did not fulfil this role. Some of them were even alleged to have taken bribes for helping in obtaining retrenchment compensation. When these complaints reached the president of the recognized union, he ruled that every application for retrenchment compensation would not be approved unless signed by him.

In the textile industry the union–worker relationship varied across departments. In the weaving department, for instance, there was a predominance of allegiance towards the unrecognized union. This union had vehemently opposed the modernization of weaving operations when it was initiated. It even resorted to violence by hiring ruffians. The management then filed a suit of unfair labour practice. It simultaneously tried to promote allegiance to the recognized union by counselling workers. However, this researcher felt that the management fell short in its efforts of directly establishing a bond with workers at the individual level.

MANAGEMENT–WORKER RELATIONSHIP

Managements everywhere have been making concerted efforts to create goodwill among employees in order to evade union influence. The engineering industry in the western region has evolved many goodwill practices such as rewarding workers for excellence in work, good attendance and good housekeeping. These are aimed at improving work morale, reducing monotony and giving a pleasant diversion from routine jobs. However, these practices can take place only if the company's financial position is sound and is bustling with business activity. With notable exceptions, the textile industry in Bombay and Ahmedabad was by and large in the shadow of industrial sickness. The management morale there was too low to give attention to building a harmonious relationship with workers.

MANAGEMENT–UNION RELATIONSHIP

In all industries covered in this study, this relationship existed on a different plane altogether. It was independent of the union–worker and worker–management relationships mentioned earlier. This was mainly due to an element of alienation existing among both of them. Being the most basic relationship for all practical purposes, the managements everywhere went out of their way to please trade union officials. They gave the latter full relief from their duties and provided them with a number of facilities. On the whole, union representatives were treated well by the managements. At times connivance with each other led to illegal and inhuman practices. In Ahmedabad, for instance, through such connivance, some workers managed to remain in the third shift permanently. Such an arrangement enabled them to run their private business during the day. Similarly, both in Ahmedabad and Coimbatore, workers were paid a single wage for working overtime, although it was against the statutory requirement of paying at the double wage rate. Known as *rokdi* (cash), this payment was a cash payment during the middle of the month and the workers were happy to receive handy cash at that time. When this researcher asked about the illegality of this practice, the managements in Coimbatore argued that they simply adhered to the practice prevailing in the region. Moreover, they pointed out that this low payment was fully compensated by giving an annual bonus of 35 to 40 per cent (of wages and dearness allowance) which was much higher than the amount decided by the statutory guideline of 8.33 to 20 per cent.

The process of technological change in textile mills at Coimbatore was smooth and undeterred by the multiplicity of unions. On an average there were eight unions per mill. Despite this, the daily operations were undisrupted only because of the management's uncompromising stand on work discipline. It was remarkable that trade union multiplicity did not result in violence which was the case in West Bengal and Maharashtra. This again was possible only because at the individual level, workers were not interested in union activities. Unlike the textile workers in Bombay and Ahmedabad, they were better off and looked healthier. Their working conditions too were much better. The researcher gathered that many of the workers in Coimbatore had their own looms at home. As such they were not keenly involved in the union–management relationship. Their attitudes towards modernization were favourable also because the sound financial position of their companies enabled them in obtaining quick gains in the form of incentive payments.

It is interesting to note here that in the textile industry in all the three regions of Ahmedabad, Bombay and Coimbatore, issues concerning technological change were negotiated at the unit level, as and when the processes were modernized. The common and major issues of wage scales and bonus were entered into only with the settlement common to the entire industry. This was settled between the Mill Owners' Association and the recognized union. The Mill Owners' Association was formed by representatives of various textile mills. The representing and recognized unions in Ahmedabad and Bombay were respectively the Mazoor Mahajan and Rashtriya Mill Mazdoor Sabha. They were the sole bargaining agents. In

Coimbatore, the workers were represented by a bargaining committee comprising representatives of a number of unions recognized in various mills.

Such a unique bargaining system is possible in the textile industry because of the uniform nature of the production process and concentration of mills in particular places. The size of the labour force in these mills, too, is more or less similar. In the engineering industry, due to such lack of uniformity, industry-wise wage settlements have never been possible.

The bargaining process in the textile industry has been a combination of 'sequential contracting' and 'contingent claims contracting'. These two terms are coined by Paul Willman (1986).[2] He applies the first term to a bargaining situation where the terms and conditions of the effort bargaining are constantly negotiated and renegotiated (as in unit-level bargaining over modernization in the present case). By the second term, namely, contingent claims contracting, Willman refers to bargaining over general terms and conditions of employment over a specified period of time. This kind of bargaining is reflected in characteristics of periodical wage settlements reached between the Mill Owners' Association and unions in the textile industry.

With the exception of one engineering concern in the western region, the incentive system was widely prevalent in the companies selected for this study. The incentive system everywhere is known to be full of problems. These are:

1. manoeuvring of output by workers and supervisors;
2. indulgence in the quota system of production;
3. inter-departmental disputes over incentive payment;
4. administrative burden.

A unique problem during automation is the upward change in production norms. The incentive amount cannot be revised proportionately because an increase in output is merely due to technological upgradation. Workers, however, refuse to accept this contribution of technology and oppose the revision in norms of production. The incentive system thus becomes a recurrent bone of contention between the union and management.

Yet the companies could not do away with the established system of incentive payment for fear of industrial unrest. However, it is noteworthy that most of the companies try to avoid an incentive system in their Greenfield plants. The management of the engineering concern in the western region had taken a policy decision of avoiding the incentive system altogether. This was in view of the company's bitter experiences in its sister plant in Bihar. Hence, instead of incentive payment linked to departmental output, the management introduced a production bonus linked with the company's total production. The production targets were based on market conditions and the projected demand for their product till the end of every financial year. The productivity linked payment was made along with 20 per cent mid-year Diwali bonus. Such advance payment was a customary practice. It was guarded by a precautionary clause in the productivity settlement. It stated that if the operatives failed to achieve the production target despite the normal working conditions, the management would make pro-rata deductions in the incentive amount from their monthly emoluments. The agreement also laid down that if there was a shortfall in the targeted production due to reasons within the management's control, the incentive amount was not to be deducted. It was not so easy to establish the cause of fall in targeted production as both the parties could blame each other. The researcher gathered that only once the production target was not fulfilled. The management, however, as a goodwill gesture, paid the amount agreed upon in the productivity settlement.

The foregoing account highlights that trade unions are only concerned with the after-effects of technological change. They negotiate over acceptance of the repercussions of modernization. They are not concerned with decisions regarding choice of technology and investments. After all it is the owners' money which will decide the affordability of technology. Interestingly, the situation in Britain is not any different. Ian Mcloughlin and Jon Clark (1994),[3] in their review of various surveys on negotiations on technological change conclude that '...in most cases, irrespective of the number of levels at which it took place, bargaining was largely restricted to employment issues, such as manning, pay, training and health and safety, and did not cover control issues or strategic issues such as investment or equipment....' (p. 105). They also found that '...on the most fundamental issues of job security and pay, unionized workforces (did) not seem to have a demonstrable advantage over their non-unionized counterparts when it (came) to negotiating technological change' (p. 126).

The gains of modernization are essentially higher productivity and better quality of products. However, mere sophisticated machinery by itself cannot fetch these results. Organizational and work culture have to be conducive to achieving high productivity and quality products. Determinants of the two facets of work culture will be analyzed in the next chapter.

REFERENCES AND NOTE

1. The history of the textile strike in Bombay lies outside the purview of this chapter. Those interested may refer to *Bombay Textile Strike, 1982–83* by H. Van Wersch, Oxford University Press, 1992.
2. **Paul Willman**, *Technological Change, Collective Bargaining and Industrial Efficiency*, Clarendon Press, 1986, pp. 85–86.
3. **Ian Mcloughlin** and **Jon Clark**, *Technological Change at Work*, Open University Press, 1994, p. 126.

7

Towards a 'Technology Friendly' Work Culture

The onus of nurturing a culture conducive to a whole-hearted acceptance of technological change and its effective implementation lies on the management. It is an integral part of the managerial prerogatives on various facets of decisions pertaining to technological change. The question arises as to what the demands of new technology are. It would be pertinent to recapitulate them here.

OPEN COMMUNICATION WITH EMPLOYEES

If an operative is sufficiently well informed in advance about the likely change in his job demands, he would be mentally prepared to accept new technology. Prior knowledge of the change would shelter him from an 'information shock' when the new machinery arrives. It would also dilute his mental stress of becoming a surplus and redundant employee.

CLOSE COORDINATION

The departments directly involved in the process of technological change are (*a*) projects, (*b*) industrial engineering, (*c*) production, and (*d*) human resource management. Decisions pertaining to choice of technology and its implementation essentially originate from the teamwork among these departments. However, in many companies covered in this study, there existed a rift between the departments of personnel and industrial engineering and production. It was a consequence of each departmental head's effort to please the union and workers and avoid taking bitter though necessary decisions in the interest of the organization.

CONTINUOUS TRAINING

While training activity should be initiated prior to the arrival of machinery, it should not be concluded after the installation of machinery. Most importantly, training should be a continuous activity. New technology demands flexibility in skills and jobs. Ongoing training makes this possible by providing employees an opportunity to hone their skills and maintain an adaptiveness conducive to change. Unfortunately, however, the importance of training had been largely ignored in companies studied in this project. Where in existence, the training activity was largely focused on workers leaving aside the middle management group. With an increasing thrust towards delayering and reduction in compartmentalization of jobs, training assumes importance as never before.

QUALITY AND PRODUCTIVITY CONSCIOUSNESS AND COST-EFFECTIVENESS

The inherent advantages of modernization, namely, a better quality product at a reduced cost, cannot come automatically with the arrival of new machinery on the shopfloor. The corresponding activities of production, namely, effective use of raw materials, energy, efficiency in work, planning and other support systems of maintenance and other service departments are prerequisites for obtaining maximum returns on investments made in new machinery. The employees at all levels are required to be sufficiently motivated to take an active interest in various jobs complementary to their own.

CUSTOMER-ORIENTED APPROACH

Customer satisfaction is not the responsibility of the marketing department alone. Any consumer looks for the right product at the right price with timely delivery. Hence in the customer satisfaction process all employees, right from the receptionist and telephone operator to managing director and from an operative to a packer are all equally involved. This value is required to be inculcated in all employees. It would be interesting to see in the following account as to how in one engineering company, the CEO had changed the existing work systems and procedures in order to fulfil the above demands of modernization.

DIRECT RAPPORT WITH EMPLOYEES

An avenue of direct rapport was opened through an information-sharing meeting between the workers and CEO. The guiding principle behind this move was the thought that if the shareholders were required to be kept informed why not the employees who directly contributed to the company's performance. Similarly, the CEO held 'coffee meetings' monthly with middle cadre employees. These obliterated the feeling of marginality among them. It is commonly observed that the middle cadre employees carry a feeling of being ignored by the management. In the present case, the CEO's meetings with the middle cadre sent signals to senior managers to share information with them as well as involve them in decision-making. The researcher felt a marked difference in the morale of these employees as compared with their counterparts elsewhere.

Various senior managers mentioned that the CEO's policy of sharing information with employees had paid rich dividends. They could feel the change in atmosphere, from mistrust to trust. As the supreme gesture of openness, the management submitted its counter-demands to the union much prior to the actual commencement of negotiations between them for arriving at a wage settlement. The management's counter-demands were followed by the department-wise meetings between union and management representatives. These had tremendous educative value.

That such an openness pays rich dividends was also observed in a textile mill in Ahmedabad. Its CEO had initiated an open door policy for employees. Any employee could approach him directly for obtaining information or grievance redressal. This had helped create a cohesive atmosphere in the organization.

IMPROVEMENT IN COORDINATION

It has been mentioned in earlier chapters that for making modernization a success, functions of production, maintenance and quality must go hand-in-hand. Simple though it appears, such well-knit teamwork does not exist in many organizations due to wrong reporting systems, over-compartmentalization and ego problems.

In an engineering organization in the south, these problems were overcome through an organizational overhaul. All the functions of production, maintenance and quality were clubbed together under the stewardship of one functional head. This arrangement facilitated speedier decision-making due to removal of various bottlenecks that had arisen from lengthier routes of communication and decision-making. More importantly, inter-departmental cross-functional teams of middle management employees were formed. This helped them to be more appreciative of the views and approaches of their colleagues and obliterated problems arising from lack of communication and understanding. The involvement of middle cadre employees in these committees contributed to their job enrichment.

Having realized that many of the communication gaps existed due to ego problems of top executives, the CEO had engaged an OD (organizational development) consultant to remove these barriers. Through organizing family gatherings and workshops for these executives, the consultant tried to create cohesiveness among them.

IMPROVEMENT IN QUALITY CONSCIOUSNESS

Towards fulfilling this objective, a functional head in this company had started a novel scheme of sending workers on educational tours to customer companies. These had helped them in understanding customer complaints and evaluating their own performance.

BUILDING CONFIDENCE AND OPTIMISM

These two basic qualities percolate from top management to the grassroots level workers and are instrumental in enhancing the morale of employees. The case of the Greenfield steel factory covered in this study supported this belief. There the commissioning of the blast furnace was delayed due to financial constraints and political problems. All the key tasks were headed by senior employees promoted from the junior management cadre. The delay in commissioning had hampered their confidence and enthusiasm. The new CEO diagnosed this problem and brought in new senior people from outside. Their fresh approach helped tremendously in boosting employee morale and achieving results.

These requirements of new technology essentially comprise the organizational culture. It is a manifestation of collective values, principles, interests and actions of people working together. These in turn, as a cumulative effect, shape the work environment, the standards of discipline, efficiency and the overall performance.

Culture at the organizational level is a sum total of the values, principles and actions of people at the individual level. Utter unconcern about the quality of output, procrastination at work and various unproductive practices are manifestations of the lack of work culture. These will be discussed later.

In the companies covered in this study, at organizational as well as individual levels, work culture varied across sectors, regions and industries. These are now discussed.

SECTORS

It is commonly observed that work culture in private sector companies is superior to that in public sector companies. The obvious reason is job security in the latter endowed by the statute. It has been instrumental in nurturing a lackadaisical work culture. Procrastination, inefficiency, rudeness and indifference towards customers are widely prevalent in public sector organizations.

An exclusive feeling of job security has resulted in the lack of accountability even among many senior management employees of public sector companies. It has been noted in chapter three as to how the process of modernization was delayed in the public sector. Lack of initiative, irresponsibility and non-commitment to jobs have been characteristic of this sector.

Government patronage to organizations in the public sector existed till the mid-eighties and early nineties. Along with liberalization, the other major step initiated by the government has been to curtail the reimbursement of cash losses. This has helped reduce the feeling of complacency among public sector executives.

Unfortunately, the public sector is viewed as 'nobody's property'. Utter disregard of housekeeping, maintenance, pilferages is common in these organizations. Very strong unionization, dilatory legal procedures and the over-protective approaches of the courts have helped in the further deterioration of work culture.

REGIONS

In India, work culture as manifested in patterns of behaviour vary across geographical regions. The level of industrialization and prosperity of industries, too, determine work behaviour. For instance, industrialization creates among people an increased consciousness of time and its productive use. Hence in cities like Bombay, despite various transport problems, people are found to be more punctual than in a small town or village. It is commonly observed that in Bihar and West Bengal even the banks do not open on time during the official business hours.

In northern states, women in government offices are often found busy knitting. Men and women while away time in drinking endless cups of tea and basking in the sun during winter. People in the south are more religious. This researcher was quite amused to see a temple within the premises of each textile mill in the southern centre of textile industry. People began their working day at office after worshipping. It was interesting to see how in a Greenfield engineering company the management organized a *pooja* (worship) every Friday during the shift change hour. The works manager used to address the workers of incoming and outgoing shifts. Being religious-minded, no worker ever dared to skip these meetings. It was the best example of the management honouring local culture and utilizing it as a communication tool to build harmony.

INDUSTRY

The financial condition of an industry has a direct bearing on the work culture. There was a remarkable difference in textile and engineering industries in this respect. Within the private sector too the prosperous mills fared better in all respects of work atmosphere and culture. Punctuality, accountability, efficiency and an overall results-oriented approach were observed in all business activities of these companies. Thus work culture and financial performance are found to be dependent upon each other.

WORK CULTURE AT THE INDIVIDUAL LEVEL

It is difficult to make a clear-cut list of what constitutes the work culture at the individual level. It is not the same as service rules or the list of duties earmarked for an employee. For instance, signing a muster on time is a service rule for a bank employee. But not indulging in small talk with a colleague while the customer is kept waiting at the counter is part of work ethics.

Akin to the definition of God in the *Upanishads* using the terminology of elimination, namely *neti neti* (not this, not this), work culture can be best conceptualized by the desirable elimination of unproductive work practices. The most commonly observed unproductive practices are now given.

Lack of Punctuality

One finds a clear-cut difference in this aspect of industrial and non-industrial organizations. In industrial organizations, punctuality is monitored through a card punching system. However, despite this, employees while away time in the canteen or rest rooms after punching 'in'. In one multinational company, employees used to punch 'in' and go to the badminton court on the company premises. The management was then forced to remove the facility altogether. In another organization, operatives in the morning shift were found to be reporting to work straight out of bed. They would then use their duty hours for shaving and bathing. In public sector steel industries, losses due to shift change delays are enormous. In order to check such practices, some managements have shifted their punching machines from the factory gates to the shop entrances where the employees are required to punch 'in' just before starting their work. In one company, the following clauses were inserted in the wage settlement itself.

1. Workmen should punch 'in' attendance after availing themselves of facilities of tea and snacks in the canteen and after changing of clothes. Only after punching 'out' the changing of clothes (at the end of the shift) should be done.
2. Punch 'in' and 'out' should be done in the respective departments and not at the factory entrance as was the case earlier.

3. When tea and dry snacks would be served in the department during shifts, there would be no interruption of work and the total time for drinking tea should not exceed ten minutes.

4. Failure to punch 'in'/'out' would be condoned on the first occasion. Wages would not be payable for the full day on each subsequent occasion of failure to punch 'in' and 'out' timings.

These conditions helped eliminate a number of unproductive practices leading to wastages of production time. More importantly, they improved manpower utilization.

In one engineering company, the management stopped the practice of serving breakfast after one hour of the commencement of the shift as it found that employees came on an empty stomach and counted time till breakfast arrived. The white collar staff, including managers, organized meetings after the breakfast time. They avoided meetings or were often late if the meetings were kept prior to serving of breakfast.

In another engineering company, the industrial engineering department found that the workers overstayed lunch break because the seating capacity of dining halls was inadequate and the dining tables were not cleaned immediately after people finished their lunch. In the subsequent wage settlement, therefore, the management started the practice of self-service in canteens and made the employees lift their plates after lunch and deposit them in the portable dish collecting stand. It could thus reduce the time lost during lunch breaks.

Attendance is kept by time offices in industrial organizations. In the Greenfield public sector steel company, the management had done away with the time office. For it had learnt from other organizational experiences that the card punching system was not above manipulations and corruption. It, therefore, started the systems of maintaining attendance registers on the shopfloor and closing factory gates fifteen minutes before the commencement of the shift. Names of employees reporting late were then communicated from the gate to the respective departmental heads. These in turn issued memos to employees and took disciplinary actions against erring employees.

Ideal though it appeared, even this system was not free from manipulations. There were cases of workers reporting at second shift timings, i.e., at 2.30 p. m. and leaving the factory premises at the end of general shift at 5.30 p. m. In a few other cases, although workers reached the factory premises on time, they did not report at their respective departments. They would call up the supervisor from elsewhere and make sure that they were marked present.

These two instances speak volumes about the tendency and capability of employees to manoeuvre any system to suit their interests. Continuous education, active involvement of unions and internalization of responsibility and commitment would reduce these erratic tendencies.

Overtime

Closely associated with attendance and time-keeping is the unproductive practice of obtaining overtime wages. It is done in connivance with union leaders, workers and supervisors. The system of overtime wage payment is cancerous. There have been instances of workers complaining to their departmental heads for not giving overtime duty while their counterparts in some other departments were availing themselves of it. In a public sector steel company, such connivance was so much out of proportion that overtime wage payment worked out to 6 per cent of the monthly emoluments of employees. It was stopped suddenly only when a new CEO issued an administrative directive to curb overtime. In another multinational engineering company, workers were used to getting about 100 overtime hours per head per month. The proportion of overtime hours to direct hours (i.e., number of hours directly utilized for jobs) worked out to 82 per cent. This meant that operatives worked only with an incentive of overtime wage payment and much of normal shift time was wasted.

Requirement for overtime work often emerges due to lacunae in managerial responsibility of production scheduling. At times there is no sufficient workload till the middle of the month. And then there is a sudden rush to fulfil the monthly target for which overtime work appears to be unavoidable.

Overtime wage payment is still considered viable when compared with the alternative of increasing employee strength on the payroll. But its disastrous effect is that the workers can easily get addicted to it. Overtime wages are affordable only when market conditions are favourable. In times of recession, however, non-availability of this payment would lead to simmering unrest and a lower employee morale. Overtime work is obviously very strenuous and stressful. Highly skilled and well-to-do workers are at times reluctant to do it. But, by and large, overtime duty is coveted.

Another example of workers' desire to work overtime was seen in a public sector engineering company. There existed a system of working on Sundays with overtime wages. It had emerged in order to fulfil the targets in March before the financial year ending. Eventually, however, the work culture deteriorated to such an extent that production targets were not reached despite working on Sundays. The incentive system proved to be meaningless because the incentive amount was virtually paid for doing the normal work supposed to be done without incentive. The Sunday overtime wage system had demoralized many of the middle management employees who had to compulsorily work on Sundays with a single wage. Strangely enough, though originally prevalent only in the month of March, the Sunday overtime system eventually started from June itself. The month of May was spared to suit the employees' leave coinciding with their children's summer holidays and family get-togethers.

In a large private sector company, mere payment of overtime wage did not induce workers to work. The supervisors then started a system of giving them additional soap bars. At the end of the shift some supervisors would merely keep the soap bars (two full bars for three workers) to induce them to continue to work in the subsequent shift. Workers would then sell these soap bars as soon as they reached the factory gates. They would thus earn about Rs 350 to Rs 400 through such sales. Despite being aware of this practice (known as 'management by soap bars'), the managers and union officials pretended to be oblivious of its repurcussions. The expenditure on soap bars ran into lakhs of rupees and was continuously on the rise. Union officials in fact justified it by saying that the Indian work system is based on 'rewards'. The official even mentioned as to how the workers sold off the safety shoes and dusters given free by the management. Having realized that it was nearly impossible for the union to check these undesirable practices, the union official merely said, 'The union has to swim with the tide!'

By and large, in continuous processes of making steel all such unproductive work practices were tolerated with the sheer objective of avoiding the nuisance value of employees. A more compelling factor was that the cost of such unproductive practices was practically irrelevant in view of the short term and immediate gains. Besides, the potential losses in the event of disruptions in the continuous flow of production were more dear and detrimental to the life of machinery.

Quota System

This is a very common unproductive practice among continuous process industries and in those industries where incentives are linked to norms of output. Workers are required to produce a fixed minimum quota of output. As the targets fixed are low, workers tend to schedule them according to their own time and speed of production. And they can still very easily fulfil the quota much prior to the scheduled time. The management is compelled to ignore whatever they do after this. Often they are found loitering, sleeping or playing cards on the shopfloor. Managements helplessly watch this waste of productive time due to employees' adamance and militant trade unionism.

In the Greenfield public sector steel factory, workers working near blast furnaces and in steel melt shops were required to take a one hour rest after each hour's work. This provision came in the wake of the factory inspectorate's directive. Yet the workers were found to be working continuously for four hours and then calling it a day.

'This is Not My Job!'

This is the most common unproductive and restrictive practice found everywhere in India as well as abroad. J. E. Mortimer (1971)[1] in his work on industries in Britain has observed that this is the most frequently complained about restrictive practice. It comprises

the insistence by a union that a certain range of work is to be carried out exclusively by its members, irrespective of whether other workers could equally well do the same work; and, conversely, the insistence by a union that its members should not be called upon to undertake certain tasks which fall outside their normal range of duties, even though they may be perfectly capable of undertaking these other tasks. (p. 71)

In India, it is not uncommon to find that a worker leaves his machine and its surrounding unclean; a mechanical maintenance operative does not touch an electric motor; a stenographer would only take dictation and type a letter but would refuse to file it—the reason being that *he is not supposed to do it.*

Procrastination

By and large, no initiative is taken unless orders are given by the superiors. Till then, tasks are conveniently 'forgotten' or postponed. If the stipulated period for taking any action is 90 days, the procedure is not initiated before the 89th day!

Why Should I Bother?

This basic attitude knowingly or unknowingly leads people to indulge in a variety of unproductive work practices. Besides, it generates new ones from time to time. Industrial operatives leave conveyor belts on during tea and lunch breaks, use compressed air as a cooler during summer only with a view to self comfort and convenience. In a textile mill, workers are found to have broken window panes for allowing fresh air to come in and thus spoiling the humidifiers.

UNPRODUCTIVITY OF STAFF

Till now we have listed the unproductive and wasteful practices associated with the manufacturing processes. Being directly linked with daily tangible performance at the shop-floor, industrial engineering experts too seem to be focusing their efforts on identifying and eliminating them. In this process, however, they tend to ignore the undesirable work practices of administrative staff and employees in service departments. Inefficiency of telephone operators, accountants and clerical staff goes unnoticed. The cricket season is a good excuse for a 'working holiday'. Delays in bills clearance, attending to telephone calls and handling official correspondence, tapping telephone conversations, speaking rudely and being indifferent to visitors and customers are some of the common malpractices.

There appears to be a lack of the conscientious attitude that 'I must do my assigned duty efficiently for I am paid to do it'. People can get away with inefficiency because of strong unionization which makes them complacent about their jobs. Further a secure employee exploits the insecure one. In a midi-steel plant, it was common among the permanent employees to sleep during duty hours and get the jobs done by contract workers merely in exchange for tea and lunch coupons. The middle management employees perforce ignored such practices because they were only concerned about *somehow* fulfilling their daily production quota. Besides, their normal tendency was not to invite trouble from union leaders.

These unproductive practices are limited to this researcher's coverage of organizations. In actuality, there must be many more depending upon the nature of the manufacturing process, sector, and region. Despite their variations, one fact is crystal clear; they retard productivity, efficiency and the overall performance. When the entire business activity is steered towards modernization, competitiveness and efficiency, these harmful practices are undesirable. Managements cannot afford to ignore them if they are to obtain maximum returns on investments. It is their prime responsibility to shed soft and compromising approaches towards maintaining discipline and efficiency. By and large, managements' efforts at eliminating such unproductive practices are not uniform across all departments. Personnel executives too have to support the shopfloor executives when the latter seek their assistance in maintaining discipline. Often in their weak efforts to appease union leaders, the personnel executives hamper the morale of middle management employees working at the shopfloor. This is an unhealthy trend creating a rift between personnel and other departments. The correct approach would be to continuously educate employees by highlighting their unproductive practices. More importantly, such an exercise should be a joint endeavour of management and union.

Work ethics have to percolate from the top. If an executive is not punctual and efficient, he cannot exercise a moral right to discipline an erring employee.

The realization that a good work culture is a prerequisite for reaping the benefits of new technology would induce all employees across all cadres to strive towards its achievement.

REFERENCE

1. **J. E. Mortimer**, *Trade Unions and Technological Change*, Oxford University Press, 1971.

8

Manpower Reduction:
The Inevitable Repercussion

As seen in the foregoing chapters, the process change in work operations renders manpower surplus and creates skill redundancy. While skill redundancy can be reduced by retraining, there is a limit to the absorption of surplus labour due to the very capacity of technology as well as business constraints. It has also been mentioned that traditionally steel and textile industries in both private and public sectors have been overmanned due to their labour intensive technology and high absenteeism rates accruing from unpleasant and hazardous nature of work. In the engineering industry, however, there has rarely been excess manpower. This is because of its requirement of skilled labour which is costly. Besides, there has been continuous upgradation of technology in most of the engineering industries. Recruitment of workers has been stopped in these companies for over a decade. Hence in the engineering companies covered in this study, there were no voluntary retirement schemes.

The case of public sector organizations, across all industries, has been quite different. Their manning levels have been kept high in pursuance of the social objective of providing employment. Overmanning curtails the productivity levels and increases the proportion of labour cost to total cost of production. Though labour is a human resource, the still bigger truth is that its economic costs cannot be ignored if the business has to survive and be profitable. It then follows that the economic objective also demands that uneconomic operations need to be closed down for preventing industrial sickness.

However, it is not at all easy to remove the surplus or even erring inefficient labour. In the statutory provision under sections 25 (N) and 25 (O) of the Industrial Disputes Act, 1947, the government's prior permission is required to be obtained for both closure of a company and reduction of labour under lay-off and retrenchment. By and large, the government is reluctant to grant permission for closure and labour reduction for any reason. As a result, many economically unviable units remain in a state of suspended animation for years. Workers are neither paid their current wages nor their legal dues which they are entitled to on termination of their service. In view of this, the Association of Chambers of Commerce had recommended deletion of the entire chapter V (B) of the Industrial Disputes Act, 1947, which contains these provisions.

The Goswami Committee which was appointed to investigate industrial sickness and suggest remedial measures for industrial restructuring also questioned the very necessity of obtaining the government's permission for retrenchment. It said that in India, due to a number of legal provisions as well as the development of case law, it is impossible for an honest employer to deviate from law when laying-off labour. At the same time, the dishonest entrepreneurs can easily get away with the said legal violations by exercising their political connections and resorting to corruption. Hence, the Goswami Committee said that in 'the best case scenario, sections 25 (N) and 25 (O) are redundant and in the worst case scenario, they are irrelevant. Hence, it makes sense to eliminate them altogether'.

While the government has encouraged modernization through various fiscal concessions, it does not easily permit retrenchment which is inevitable during the process of modernization. To overcome this problem, the government had been contemplating since 1992 to introduce an Exit Policy. However, there was no explicit statement on this policy. Even the public statements by political leaders and ministers were vague and changed to suit political exigencies. Undeterred by their unpredictability, as a via media to reducing manpower, private sector companies have been introducing Voluntary Retirement Schemes (VRS) (also termed as Golden Handshake).

The Voluntary Retirement Schemes have varied across industries. These are now described.

STEEL

The problem of surplus manpower in the integrated steel company in the private sector surfaced when the steel melt shop II was shut down in 1983. It was then that a VRS was formally introduced. The following conditions were required to be fulfilled to be entitled to the scheme.

1. Employees were rendered surplus on account of rationalization/reorganization of the labour force.
2. It was possible to abolish the employee's post or a post down the line.
3. It was possible to absorb a surplus employee in the vacancy caused due to voluntary retirement of the employee or two steps down the line [of hierarchy] but not in the lowest category of unskilled workers.

The scheme offered an ex-gratia payment and other benefits. Earlier, a near relative of a permanent employee who completed 25 years of service would have been entitled for a placement in the company. This benefit was protected even under the voluntary retirement scheme provided the employee would have put in, if not actually, at least notionally, 25 years of service had he been superannuated in the normal course. In addition, the benefits of free medical service for himself, spouse and dependent parents and also concessional points of consideration for allotment of quarters as admissible to all retired employees were continued.

Yet the scheme did not receive wide acceptance. During the first eight years of its introduction, only 146 employees had retired voluntarily. The scheme was not popular because the ex-gratia payment was not considered very attractive. Moreover, it was offered with a touch of secrecy only to unwanted employees by the concerned managers. Some managers were reluctant to fulfil the condition of abolishing the posts although they did not much object to reducing the number of employees in these posts. The acceptance of VRS was considered to be a stigma and the employees seemed to have preferred to protect their status of being an employee of the prestigious company rather than sitting idle at home.

As the modernization process accelerated and the problem of surplus manpower became serious, the company once again revised the scheme in 1994. It offered an increased compensation equivalent to one-and-a-half month's salary for each completed year of service or monthly salary at the time of retirement multiplied by the balance months of service left before the date of the employee's retirement on superannuation (60 years), whichever was lower. In any case the amount of compensation would not exceed Rs 5 lakhs.

It is noteworthy that the revised scheme deleted the earlier provision of employment for the dependent. It also removed the provision for allotment of company's accommodation and explicitly stated that the payment under the scheme would be made only after the employee handed over the company's accommodation. This scheme is only for those declared as surplus employees. The declaration is left entirely at the discretion of the company. This discretion is maintained because in some multinational companies when an attractive VRS package was kept open to all, the company lost both skilled people and also incurred huge cost in compensation.

There has been a further refinement in the scheme in 1995 in view of the impending automation. Known as the Early Separation Scheme, this too is granted entirely at the discretion of the management.

Under this scheme, a monthly pension scheme has been introduced for those employees separating before attaining the age of 40 years and who have not completed ten years of service as on the date of separation. They will be entitled to get a monthly pension equivalent to last salary drawn by them till their attaining the age of superannuation. For those employees working for over ten years but separating before crossing the age of 45 years and those who have crossed 45 years the scheme offers an attractive pension respectively of 1.25 times and 1.5 times of their last drawn salary at the time of retirement.

In the event of death of the separating employee within the pension period, his nominee too will get the full monthly pension till the scheduled date of superannuation. The separation scheme also provides for medical facility in the company's hospital and other benefits such as a house rent grant or education grant for children. Another important entitlement for those separating and desirous of starting some business is a refundable loan of Rs 2 lakhs or 50 per cent of the total pension benefits, whichever is less.

It is noteworthy that these separation benefits are given only after the separating employee vacates the company's accommodation. This provision indicates the employee's tendency to encroach upon the company's accommodation. The scheme is made attractive further by providing for a lucky draw for a group of every 500 employees. The first three prizes offered through this lottery are a chassis of a truck, a jeep or a car.

The nature of this scheme speaks volumes about the quantum of surplus manpower (the details of which were not made available to this researcher). And the personnel executives too did not seem to have a precise idea of the number of surplus employees. It also gives some idea about the huge potential of the impending technological change which will make it difficult to absorb the manpower likely to be rendered surplus. It therefore has removed the provision of employment for the dependents which existed in the original VRS scheme introduced in 1983.

Unlike the private sector company, the public sector company had a constraint of funds for compensating those who opted to retire voluntarily. It had therefore coincided its modernization programme with a mass retirement of workers in 1993–94. Nearly 4,500 employees were going to retire during that year. Simultaneously, recruitments were reduced to 2:1 proportion. It meant that when two vacancies were created in the unskilled category, only one was filled through redeployment or recruitment.

The public sector company did offer a voluntary retirement scheme eventually when the central government created a National Renewal Fund in the 1991–92 union budget. It was a safety net for those employees to be retrenched due to technology upgradation. It offered 45 days salary for every completed year of service or the remaining years of service whichever was less. It was found that when kept open to all, good employees who were sure of getting employment outside or were capable of being self-employed jumped at the scheme. The invalid and inefficient lingered on. Hence, the management introduced a clause reserving its discretion in offering the voluntary retirement scheme to an employee.

In the midi-steel company in the private sector the problem and extent of surplus manpower was not so severe as in the integrated steel companies mentioned earlier. However, in view of the need for continuous modernization in the near future, the company has taken a policy decision to reduce recruitment by:

1. stopping employment of 'sons of the soil'.
2. stopping employment of employees' sons.
3. filling up the 'Badli (substitute) Workers' Pool' through employment exchanges and avoiding keeping them on the payroll for more than 240 days which is the statutory minimum period for confirming permanency of service till superannuation.

How voluntary are the Voluntary Retirement Schemes? It is difficult to answer this question with precise statistics. But newspaper reports and case law do indicate that at times managements do exercise 'involuntary' pressure on employ-ees to accept voluntary retirement. Courts have condemned these practices and directed the managements to reinstate such employees without discontinuity in service. In Blue Star Ltd (as reported in *Maharashtra Times*, 23 September 1993) an employee, Mr Krishna Hedulkar, was informed about the voluntary retirement scheme and was even asked to sign his resignation papers. The management then gave him a cheque of compensation for Rs 2.5 lakhs. Mr Hedulkar, however, did not deposit this cheque in the bank and filed a complaint in the industrial court alleging his forced resignation from service. The industrial court decided the case in favour of Mr Hedulkar. The company then filed an appeal in the High Court. During the court proceedings, the management agreed that the VRS was not conveyed with prior notification and publicity. Besides Mr Hedulkar had 12 years of service ahead and there was no enquiry pending against him. Such being the case, the court wondered as to who would prefer to surrender their remaining service merely for Rs 2.5 lakhs. Thus the court dismissed the management's appeal and ordered the reinstate-ment of Mr Hedulkar.

It has been mentioned earlier that managements have retained their discretionary power in deciding an employee's application for the VRS. The Karnataka High Court questioned this discretion in P. Adishesha Reddy and others V. Bharat Gold Mines Ltd and Another (1993, ILLJ, 379). In this case, the management had refused permission to grant availing of the VRS to the applicants. The latter then filed a writ petition and argued that unless the voluntary retirement was prohibited by the service regulations, refusal of permission to voluntary retirement amounted to arbitrary action without authority of law. In its defense, the management stated that the question of granting permission to retire voluntarily arose only when the staff was surplus. Besides the management also stated that it was in financial difficulties. Hence, it feared that even if the petitioners' case was considered favourably on humanitarian grounds, hundreds of other employees would come forward with similar applications, which would push the company deeper into loss. The High Court, however, dismissed the management's plea. It observed that in service jurisprudence, voluntary retirement is the choice given to employees just as the employers have been conferred with the choice of compulsory retirement. Hence the employer is duty bound to accept the employee's request. Otherwise, the court ruled, the refusal amounted to compelling a person to work against his will and hence constituted forced labour. The court also observed that in the given case, voluntary retirement was not sought with a view to escape any enquiry for serious offences, or to escape order of suspension or to escape liability for loss caused to management. In view of all these reasons, the court allowed the petition and directed the management to pay the applicants their entitlements under the scheme.

VOLUNTARY RETIREMENT SCHEME IN THE TEXTILE INDUSTRY

Known as the Retrenchment Compensation (RC) Scheme in the textile industry, the compensation package is not so attractive as in other industries. Depending upon the capacity to pay, the private sector mills in Bombay have paid 21 to 25 days wages (as against the statutory minimum of 15 days) for every completed year of service. In Ahmedabad, the managements paid legal dues of retrenchment and ex-gratia amount for every completed year of service. The ex-gratia amount was decided through negotiations. Workers in these mills seemed to be quite keen to accept the compensation and leave the job. Often those who opted for retrenchment outnumbered the number of posts to be absorbed. As their application for RC were required to be forwarded through the union, there were reports of union representatives being bribed for recommending their names.

The scheme was first offered in 1988 in some of the private mills in Bombay which had survived the textile strike. They were now keen to reduce manpower to facilitate modernization. Unlike in the NTC mills, surplus workers in private mills are not paid idle wages. They have no other option but to leave the company. After years of monotonous and strenuous jobs they appeared to be eager to receive the lumpsum amount and invest it in agriculture or a small business. In the private mill covered in this study, the strength of employees came down from 10,642 in 1988 to 4,388 in 1993. The majority of employees opting for RC were weavers. And the reason possibly being that compared to their colleagues from other departments they had better job prospects outside. They were also more confident of starting weaving business on a small scale. When the RC was introduced in textile mills, there was an initial exodus of weavers which created a skill imbalance in the mills. The management then introduced a proviso to use its discretionary power while allowing applications for voluntary retirement.

A voluntary retirement scheme cannot be effected without cooperation from the union. In the textile industry union involvement is very decisive in deciding the number of posts to be abolished. The management is required to give notice of change to the union for the proposed plan of retrenchment. No decision is taken without the union's consent. The workers opting for VRS have to tender resignations only through the recognized union. It has already been mentioned that this practice led to corruption. By an agreement, in Bombay and

Ahmedabad respectively 5 and 2 per cent of retrenchment compensation per employee was paid directly to the recognized unions in the private sector. In NTC mills in Bombay this percentage was lower (3 per cent) whereas in Ahmedabad there was no such difference between private and public sector mills. Despite such arrangements, retrenchment proposals were not easily agreed upon. In some cases the period of negotiation varied from one-and-a-half to two years. In these companies the modernization process could not be commissioned even after the arrival of new machinery.

A private sector mill in Ahmedabad avoided such problems by making an advance payment of 2 per cent of compensation per employee to the recognized union. The management was confident of its direct rapport with workers and hence avoided union interference through this act. This company was making losses of Rs 45 lakhs per month and was on the verge of liquidation. Hence it took a sudden decision to close down its process house and the folding department. The CEO met the workers personally and told them the circumstances compelling this move. They were paid post-dated cheques of their dues and were asked not to come to work from the next day. Workers had faith in the management and were convinced of the genuine business difficulties. This example once again reiterates the fact that the management–worker relationship is independent of the management–union relationship.

In the engineering and textile mills of the south there was no practice of giving unions a share of workers' retrenchment compensation by the management.

As mentioned earlier, payment of RC in NTC mills has been facilitated through the National Renewal Fund. It offers one-and-a-half month's wages for every completed year of service or for the remaining years of service, *whichever is less*. This proviso safeguards the management's interest. However, this scheme evoked a poor response from workers in NTC mills because they get full monthly wages by merely signing the muster rolls and sitting idle on the mill premises.

The National Renewal Fund was originally also set up for providing counselling and placement services for re-employment of the displaced workers and retraining them for facilitating their redeployment. In practice, however, the fund was released for payment of retrenchment compensation and the above objective was sidelined in the debate over closure of mills. It is noteworthy that the government encouraged retrenchment by prompt release of funds whenever managements forwarded applications for the same. Yet on the other hand, the very same government did not readily give financial assistance to buy cotton and pay for operational costs of mills. As one of the steps in promoting liberalization, the government also stopped reimbursement of cash losses. To overcome this problem, some NTC mills in Bombay decided to keep the machinery running at least by selling yarn to suppliers of cotton and earning conversion charges. But the union opposed this move for reasons best known to the leaders themselves.

The issue of closure of terminally sick textile mills has been caught up in the cobwebs of bureaucracy and political exigencies. The crux of the problem was whether the mills should be allowed to sell their surplus land to raise funds for settling legal dues of workers and invest in modern machinery for restarting the closed mills. This issue has remained unsolved to date.

How rehabilitative has been the lumpsum amount paid as retrenchment compensation to workers? There is no authentic data available on this aspect of the voluntary retirement schemes. Managements cannot be asked to look after this aspect of the employee welfare. It is the trade union's responsibility to educate their members on the productive use of compensation. They could even set up small business/ancillary units of small groups of retired employees. Efforts in this direction are lacking. It was gathered during discussion with workers and their union representatives that in the textile industry, most of them had used the compensation in clearing their debts or for marrying off their daughters.

In any modernization process, the generation of manpower surplus is inevitable. The choice of technology cannot be such as to avoid manpower reduction. This has been the experience of companies worldwide. The prime responsibility of the management lies in moving with the times by continuously upgrading its technology and re-engineering systems. Bitter and unpleasant tasks of retrenchment should be preferred to industrial sickness and ultimate closures. Voluntary organizations and trade unions should come forward to promote productive uses of retrenchment compensation and make retrenchment less painful. This would in turn generate some employment and contribute towards economic development in a small way.

Along with reduction of manpower surplus, the new technology demands an efficient utilization of the existing human resources. Only the motivated employees can be efficient and committed. This realization has ushered in new practices in human resource management and industrial relations. These are presented in the next chapter.

REFERENCE

1. **Omkar Goswami**, Report of the Committee of Industrial Sickness and Restructuring, Ministry of Finance, Government of India, 1993.

9

New Trends in Industrial Relations: Their Implications for Modernization

A sound industrial relations system is a precondition for the origin, survival and progress of any business activity. The latter in turn cannot flourish without continuous modernization. Hence as we move towards higher levels of industrialization, the nexus between industrial relations and the success of modernization becomes more prominent. In the present chapter, we shall analyze this link at the outset.

The field of industrial relations is very dynamic. Being deeply rooted in the economic relationship between employer and employee, it is also sensitive to the developments and demands of business activity. It is the economic well-being of business which determines the direction of industrial relations. The management of an economically sound business can afford to concede to demands of a higher wage and bonus. Similarly, when the employment level is high and jobs are secure, unions can wield more power. In converse situations of recession and industrial sickness, even a just demand by workers cannot be considered and the power of unions is eroded. A universal historical account traced from the early days of industrialization proves this nexus between economic conditions and industrial relations. The case of India is no exception to this. D. R. Gadgil (1938)[1] notes,

The years 1919 to 1921 were the most prosperous years for the new labour movement in India. The industries had been generally doing well and the manufacturers were anxious not to lose many working days during the boom period. The wage level had also lagged considerably behind the general prices and there was, therefore, a large margin left for increments. This period was, therefore, one of generally short and on the whole successful strikes.... The (trade union) movement began with a series of successful strikes during the upward curve of the trade cycle and rapidly increased in numbers and strength. With the advent of an adverse period a great many of these mushroom growths perished, and the whole movement was for a time at a very low level of membership and funds (pp. 286–87).

Prosperity and depressive economic conditions found to occur in cycles have been termed as trade cycles in the western literature on economics. The nexus between the trade cycle and industrial relations is a well-established truth. David Coats (1989)[2] writes, 'Economic success, while it lasts, bolsters the self-confidence of skilled and organized sections of the working class and keeps alive the tradition and experiences of industrial militancy, if not of political radicalism' (p. 170). The British experience bears testimony to the relationship between strikes and the level of employment. Ken Coats and Tony Topham (1980)[3] observe that

> The one durable period of full employment in our history from 1940 to 1967 was characterized by relatively large numbers of small, short, unofficial strikes. These had no economic significance, though they were heavy with social and political meaning. The most severe and prolonged period of unemployment, from 1929 to 1937 was the nearest to 'industrial peace' which had been experienced in the 20th century, and it has usually been assumed that experience of unemployment is a deterrent to strike action (p. 217).

Concomitantly, strikes are also caused due to inflationary conditions and insecurity arising from initial stages of recession and technological change.

Akin to trade cycles have been the cycles of union approaches to management. They have passed through the cycles of low levels of unionization and submissions to high militancy and deunionization. This has been analyzed by this author[4] in her earlier writings. These show that during the nascent period of industrialization, when the owners were very powerful, organizing workers was an uphill task. The prerequisite of seven members for establishing a union, as laid down by the Trade Union Act, 1926, shows that bringing together even such a small number of workers was not easy and hence a rare phenomenon. The post-independence period, too, is marked by such cycles. After the initial normalcy with occasional disruptions from 1947 to the early sixties, trade union actions since the late sixties to early eighties are marked by high militancy and violence.

The long-drawn Bombay textile strike has in many ways changed the course of industrial relations. It has ushered in an increased assertiveness on the part of the management. The management's right to manage is now reflected in their practice of placing counter-demands. It originally emerged in the Bombay–Pune region and then moved on to other regions. Interestingly, while the managements in Bombay and Pune openly talked about their counter-demands, elsewhere, their counterparts appeared to be hesitant in discussing this 'unusual' practice.

The management's right to manage is explicitly mentioned in decisions pertaining to technological change. As mentioned in earlier chapters, they are well-guarded prerogatives of management, reiterated in consecutive wage settlements. For instance, in a wage settlement in one enterprise signed in 1994 between the union and management, the following rights of the company have been explicitly mentioned.

1. The company shall be entitled to set up standards for jobs (time standards) and to decide upon recruitment, selection, promotion, deployment, allotment of shifts, working hours, holidays and transfer from one section, department or division to another as the case may be.

2. The company shall be entitled to eliminate, change or consolidate jobs, sections, departments or divisions provided that the union is kept informed about the company's decisions and provided further that when the workmen's monetary interests, in the opinion of the union, are likely to be adversely affected, the union shall have the right to represent the individual cases to the company.

3. The company shall be entitled to plan, direct and control operations of the plants, to introduce new or improved products and production methods, to establish production and quality standards and to effect technological developments, which, at its sole discretion, would lead to better utilization of machines and increase in productivity.

4. The company shall be entitled to make such rules and regulations as it may consider necessary for the conduct of its business and for maintaining order and safety in the operation of the company's work.

5. The company shall be entitled to deduct wages on the basis of '**No Work No Pay**' in the event of the workmen failing to discharge their responsibilities or refusing to carry out the work entrusted to them without any justifiable reason.

The counter-demands of the management are reflected in the following clauses of another settlement.

1. The union shall not encourage or condone absenteeism, acts of theft, willful damage to the company's property, violence, sabotage, *gherao*, go-slow or any other act of misconduct.

2. The workmen shall keep their machines and work places clean and tidy.

3. A workman shall inspect his own jobs, be responsible for minor maintenance of the machine he is working on, shall also assist maintenance crews during machine/ equipment breakdowns and shall monitor gauges, toolings, instruments, etc., used by him for periodic checking and calibration.

4. All workmen shall sign the daily time and production booking sheets at the end of their respective shifts in confirmation of the quantity of the output produced by

them. The quantity of output produced by workmen would be certified by their superiors. Failure to do so or reporting wrong figures of productions would make the operatives liable for disciplinary action.

These clauses, while reflecting the management's assertiveness, also highlight the new approach of management. It expresses trust in employees' capabilities on the one hand and makes them accountable for the quantity and quality of their assigned work. Workers in this company are trained to check the quality of their output on the line itself. A successful continuation of this practice may perhaps result in dispensing with quality inspectors and supervisors in the future. Apart from their noble objective of job enrichment, these clauses are also indicative of the shift towards imposition of responsibility on trade unions.

Responsible trade unionism is necessitated by the increased market competition induced by economic liberalization. It follows then that harmonious industrial relations must prevail if the returns on investment in capital-intensive technology are to be gainfully achieved. Having realized this, managements are now making concerted efforts to establish a direct rapport with employees instead of concentrating only on maintaining good relations with the union. They are thus shedding their approach of 'arm's length dealing' with workers. Some of the new practices, as observed in the companies under study, are now detailed.

Arranging Company Visits by Employees' Family Members

This is obviously aimed at establishing a bond with employees' families and softening an element of alienation between the organization and its employees. It would be interesting to note here that in pursuance of this objective, a multinational engineering company started dispatching its house magazine directly to the employees' residences.

The company welfare activities are now extended also to workers' families. This is done through felicitations of their children who excel in academic and extra-curricular activities. The family members are linked to the organization through subcontracting of jobs to wives of employees. These jobs vary from stitching of uniforms and making writing pads from one-sided computer paper, supplying food to the canteens to assembling electronic components.

Awarding Employees

No act other than recognition of employees performance would be more gratifying. In view of this, an engineering company has instituted a 'Man of the Month' Award for recognizing the performance of the outstanding employees. The criteria of selection have been: (*a*) good attendance, (*b*) quality and quantum of work output, (*c*) discipline, (*d*) machine upkeeping, (*e*) cooperation with colleagues, (*f*) observance of safety regulations, (*g*) overall shop presentation and (*h*) outstanding achievements in and outside the job.

The 'Man of the Month' is given a memento, a certificate of merit and Rs 100 in a special informal function held on the shopfloor in the first week of every month. More importantly, the photographs of all the awardees are displayed on notice boards all over the company. Thus both monetary and non-monetary ways of recognizing good performance have been beautifully combined in this award. In other organizations covered in this study, not all these parameters of recognition were combined. They had separate rewards for good attendance and housekeeping.

Improvement in Communication

Managements are increasingly recognizing the value of open and direct communication with their employees. By doing this, they wish to remove the barriers often created by union members. In one company, along with the house magazine a monthly wall journal has been started. Published on poster paper of about 4' × 4' size, it is pasted at all strategic points such as near water coolers, canteen entrances and change rooms. The wall journal keeps the employees informed about the achievements of their company and colleagues in technical areas. News regarding cultural and sports events of national importance is also communicated through the wall journals.

In view of establishing direct communication the CEO in one engineering company in the south has started meeting all employees once a year. This meeting is similar to the annual general meeting of shareholders. The CEO shares with employees information about the company, its performance and future plans. Interestingly, the CEO also meets the middle management employees once a month. Known as 'Coffee Meetings', these have contributed positively towards improving employee morale.

In some companies after a spell of disturbed industrial relations, the management realized in introspection that its personnel department had failed in settling employees grievances promptly. The personnel officers had lost touch with employees and were concerned only with dealing with union representatives. It therefore reorganized the structure of its personnel department and posted a personnel officer in each department. These officers were directed to help employees in prompt settlement of their grievances.

It is now well recognized that workers' involvement in work-related activities helps bond them emotionally to the company and thereby reduce alienation. Apart from the statutory works committees or joint management councils, there is an increasing trend towards establishing quality circles. They are essentially participatory forums and promote team spirit among employees.

However, experience of companies (in this study) about the functioning of quality circles was not very positive. In some companies, workers' initial enthusiasm about quality circles waned. They found the suggestion scheme more attractive because it brought them individual recognition as well as cash award when the management accepted their suggestion. Another reason for the decline in interest towards quality circles was the changed preference of the top management. When the CEO's interest is visibly noticed, employees too take an active interest. Quality circles give a pleasant diversion from routine work. But in some cases workers misused the facility given by the management for organizing quality circle meetings. Supervisors complained that too much of production time was wasted in the name of quality circle meetings. 'If the workers were made to organize these meetings only during lunch breaks or after shift hours, would they show this much interest?' a supervisor questioned. Workers in this company were attending the quality circle meetings during their overtime work period.

Suggestion schemes and quality circles were non-existent in the textile industry. This fact re-emphasizes our observation that it is sound economic position alone that would give impetus to all such activities aimed at promoting goodwill. Industrial sickness and uncertainty in terms of job security cast a shadow on the employees' interest in these activities.

Suggestion schemes remained on paper also in those industries where union–management relations were estranged. This brings home the point that 'goodwill schemes' are essentially peace time activities. Unless the management is perceived to be fair, employees cannot be induced to participate in joint endeavours. A basic 'we feeling' towards the company is essential for motivating the employees towards participation.

Organizing Cultural Programmes, Sports Activities and Health Camps

These too are aimed at promoting goodwill among employees and reducing their monotonous routine of life. The annual health camps strengthen the feeling that the company cares for its employees.

In many ways these practices act as 'Hygiene Factors' to borrow Herzberg's[5] term. By themselves they do not ensure industrial peace; yet their presence promotes harmonious relations between management and employees. And more importantly, they take root only in a cordial atmosphere at the work place.

That financial stakes in business would nurture a feeling of ownership is quite natural. Feeling of ownership outvalues mere participation in ultimate results. In view of this, Employee Stock Ownership Plans (ESOP) were introduced in some organizations covered in this study. However, to the researcher's surprise, these schemes did not bring about the expected results. Unproductive work practices were not reduced; nor was the intensity of animosity among the workers belonging to two different divisions of the same company. When questioned about this paradox, the trade union leaders commented that the company's shares were bought because they were bonus shares at a special concessional price. Besides these were viewed as yet another share market transaction aimed at making money. For the employees were free to sell these shares after three years.

In recognition of the importance of goodwill and the essentiality of ESOP, managements abroad have been enthusiastically pursuing them. They are found to provide a sound foundation for implementing technological change successfully. John Bessant (1993)[6] has categorized the dimensions of these changed practices under two spheres: work organization and management organization. In the first category, he placed 'changes in job title, team working, greater responsibility for quality and machine maintenance, an involvement in continuous improvements and responsibility for sequencing work processes' (p. 197). Multi-skilled team working was another common feature in the companies Bessant studied. Changes in reward systems too were instrumental in effective implementation of new technology. The change oriented dimensions of management organization, as observed by Bessant, were flatter organizational structures, change in service conditions, including status and management–union relationships, control structures and loosening the boundaries between functional departments. These companies increasingly emphasized achieving shared purposes and values of Total Quality Management and Just In Time. Bessant also found an increased importance given to continuous training and development.

The enthusiastic response to Employee Stock Ownership Plans reiterates that worker ownership is the highest state of participation. In India, a pioneering experiment was initiated through the workers' takeover of the Kamani Tubes Ltd (KTL) in 1988. The workers of KTL, who were not paid their wages for over three years, offered to take over their sick factory which was on the verge of closing down. They approached the Board for Industrial and Financial Reconstruction (BIFR) with the said proposal. The BIFR responded favourably and directed the Industrial Development Bank of India to act as the operating agency for putting the proposal into effect.

At the outset, the workers agreed for a wage freeze for the first three years and also deferment of annual wage increments for the initial two years. The financial institutions gave a helping hand by liberalizing recovery of outstanding dues. Unfortunately, however, the revival package could not cure industrial sickness mainly because of the 'weak and inadequate executive and managerial cadre'. Other reasons included 'crash in international copper prices and erosion of working capital' (for details please see Corporate Dossier of *The Economic Times*, 22–28 September 1995). Subsequently, the BIFR has expressed dissatisfaction and decided to take over the company.

As mentioned earlier, a trend of deunionization has already been established in different countries. As the wage levels have risen, workers are not interested in attending union meetings. Peter Hain (1986)[7] writes about this scenario in Britain:

Union branch meetings are poorly attended. On average less than one tenth of union members now turn up regularly to branch meetings—roughly 2 per cent of the national electorate. The most active members form an even smaller proportion, so that their claims to represent the working class can be questioned, especially since only a half of workers are registered union members. When it comes to undertaking strike action this problem can become acute and certainly acts as a brake on union militancy (p. 308).

There has been a severe decline of about 4 million in trade union membership in Britain in 1991 from an all time record of 13.3 million in 1979.[8] Legislative changes including the end of the closed shop (meaning a union-membership agreement between employer and union wherein union membership is an absolute condition of employment in the shop[9]) have been instrumental towards this situation. From closed shop there has been a shift towards union free workplaces in the UK. Philip Bassett (1986)[10] mentions the employment practices adopted by Greenfield organizations like International Business Machines (UK). These are:

1. 'refusal to recognize unions, not because of their potential nuisance value, but because their collectivism runs wholly counter to the company's fundamentally individualist philosophy',
2. three beliefs, as essence of its corporate culture, namely, respect for the individual, service to the customer and the pursuit of excellence,
3. a lifetime job security,
4. removal of status barriers among employees of different cadres by giving a common dining facility and other benefits,
5. a recognition that any employee can contribute towards the development of the company and hence there is an equal opportunity for all,
6. wages are decided not collectively but through performance assessment and the opportunity for an employee to improve his performance well before the yearly review,
7. open communication between the managerial and non-managerial employees and regular checks on the system through extensive internal opinion surveys.

There is an increasing thrust towards signing of single-union deals in Britain. A single union deal comprises 'most or all of the following elements: single-status conditions, a company council, flexibility agreements, no-strike agreement and pendulum arbitration' (Gregor Gall and Sonia Mckay, 1994, 446).[11]

In pendulum arbitration, the arbitrator accepts *in toto* the position of either of the parties and will not derive a compromise formula, when a disputant is aware that his unjustifiable demand will force the arbitrator to accept his opponent's position, he may naturally put forth only reasonable demands in the first instance itself. As an integral part of a strike-free agreement, pendulum arbitration has become quite popular in the UK.

The above-mentioned approaches are widely termed as Human Resource Management (HRM) approaches. These, according to Storey (1992)[12] 'are designed to elicit employee commitment and develop resourceful humans' (*op. cit.* 12). The focus of implementing these has been shifted from the personnel department to the shop. Ian Mcloughlin and Jon Clark (1994)[13] observe that in the USA and Australia there is an increasing realization that adversarial union–management approaches do not facilitate effective implementation of new technology. The changed approaches pertain to the employers' initiative in shaping a cooperative relationship with employees which often involve 'exclusion of trade unions through either the practice of non-union human resource management or the weakening of union bargaining positions in unionized environments' (p. 225). In the Australian case, as these authors have observed, under the influence of European models of social partnership, there is union-based employee involvement and participation in technological change.

In recognition of the value of employee participation and the new approach towards human resource management, yet another unique experiment of management–union partnership was initiated in the USA. In 1982, General Motors realized the constraints in manufacturing a small car under the existing Memorandum of Agreement with the United Auto Workers Union (UAWU). It, therefore, set up another subsidiary known as the Saturn Corporation. It is basically a partnership organization wherein the work structure is team based. These teams comprise 6 to 15 members. 'They are self-directed and empowered with the authority, responsibility and resources necessary to meet their day-to-day assignments and goals including producing to budget, quality, housekeeping, safety and health, maintenance, material and inventory control, training, job assignments, repairs, scrap control, vacation approvals, absenteeism, supplies, recordkeeping, personnel selection and hiring, work planning, and work scheduling' (Rubinstein Saul, et al.).[14]

The Saturn experiment has gone beyond the conventional union–management participatory forums. Apart from the normal off-line labour management committees and teams, as well as on-line self-directed work groups, systems of on-line co-management by the union have been developed. Rubinstein et al. observe that in this unique system 'union leaders have been partnered with non-represented Saturn employees through a joint selection process to carry out new roles as operations middle management replacing the foremen, general foremen and superintendents found in traditional GM plants'.

Work teams organized into modules in Saturn have two advisors jointly selected by the management and union. One of them represents the UAWU. These advisors are not involved in the recruitment process or disciplinary matters. They are concerned with the organization of work and resource management. The union is also involved in selection of retailers and sales representatives. The union further took initiative in starting a

bottom-up planning process to identify problems that limited productivity, quality and profitability. Over a six-week period work units identified 1,150 specific action items and presented these to Saturn's president and his top leadership team. One outgrowth of this process and related research was the realization that Saturn lacked an effective off-line problem-solving system for issues that involved multiple work groups or required joint action from the work units, middle management, and Saturn's engineering professionals. At the union's initiative, a two day meeting was held with the union leadership team and a cross-section of Saturn executives representing engineering and operations. [This problem-solving activity]...provided an opportunity for engineering management and union leaders to reaffirm their joint interest in solving quality problems. Local union representatives are now working together with Saturn engineering and operations management to implement an integrative off-line problem-solving process throughout the organization (p.351).

As for the conflicts that emerge in the joint forums at Saturn, Rubinstein *et al.* observe that these are not clear cut, bilateral labour versus management conflicts. Instead, they often involve multiple groups with different interests and perspectives. (Instead of resolving these conflicts) through a single negotiated agreement or unilateral decision, they are subjected to a more extended set of discussions, often taking place in multiple forums until either a consensus emerges or a crisis forces a final decision (p. 353). Such consensus leads the decision-makers to a 'shared commitment (to implementation) and reinforces the value and principles on which Saturn was built' (p.354).

What have been the achievements of this unique experiment? The usual parameters of this assessment are 'continuous improvements in productivity, costs, profitability, market share and the time it [an organization] takes to bring new products to market'. The authors note that while in Saturn, both the management and the local union are held accountable for performance, the success of this experiment lies in its transferring of over 400 technical and process innovations to other divisions of General Motors (p. 364). Besides, its image as 'A Different Kind of Car—A Different Kind of Company' and its quality performance have boosted GM's public relations and the market value.

Rubenstein *et al.* rightly point out that although the Saturn experiment embodies 'best practices in high performance manufacturing' (p. 368), it leaves out the issue of providing 'equivalent voice and representation to the white-collar, middle management, professional and technical workers who lie outside the UAWU's jurisdiction or beyond the coverage of existing labour law' (p.368).

This case study does not touch upon the issues and modalities of sharing of financial responsibilities between the union and management. Although Saturn is a wholly owned subsidiary corporation of General Motors, how are the profits shared? In the event of losses, what will be the union's liabilities? These questions remain unanswered. A probe into these issues will help in drawing lessons for India. For the importance of 'economic motivators' cannot be overlooked in the case of union–management dynamics in the Indian industrial relations system.

In many ways, the Saturn experiment is an ideal case even in the US scenario where workers' interest in the unions is waning mainly because of their economic well-being. The traditional relationship between the union and management everywhere has been that of conflict emerging from a clash of interest. As the nations move towards industrial maturity, they increasingly feel the necessity to develop a team spirit with workers and their unions. They seem to have realized that in the absence of good human relations, no capital investment in sophisticated machinery would enhance productivity and quality. In pursuit of this objective, various forms of participation varying from works committees to quality circles and from employee shareholding to worker representation on the board of directors have been tried in various parts of the world.

The US Commission

The level of industrialization and the subsequent change in the nature of the labour force require a change in labour–management relations. Having realized this, the Clinton government in the USA appointed a Commission on the Future of Worker–Management Relations in 1993.[15] It submitted a Fact-Finding Report in May 1994 and Recommendations in December 1994. It aimed at investigating the current status of worker–management relations with reference to changes to be brought about in the legal framework and practice of collective bargaining to facilitate direct resolution of conflict by the parties themselves and enhance productivity through labour–management cooperation.

The US Economy

At the outset, one must see the relevant parameters of the US economy which caused concern and were instrumental in the setting up of the Commission. The most prominent factor among these was the slow growth rate of labour productivity, about 2.5 per cent per year. A fall in the growth rate of GDP per employee, from 2.6 per cent (1950–1973) to 0.5 per cent (1973–1992), has given alarming signals. The ratio of net imports to GDP was 0.094 in 1960. In 1991, it rose to 0.214. For over a decade from the eighties to early nineties, the US ran a substantial trade deficit in its national accounts. It moved during this period from being the world's greatest creditor to the world's greatest debtor nation.

There has been an overall change in the structure of employment in the USA—from manufacturing to the service sector. Within the service sector too there has been a change of manufacturing skill requirement. Technological advancement has brought about a shift towards white collar jobs. It has also reduced the distance between jobs of workers and of supervisors. The proportion of women in the workforce has been on the rise from 33.9 per cent in 1950 to 57.9 per cent in 1993. These changes determine the nature of labour–management relations and collective bargaining. They also shape their expectations from each other. Against this backdrop, the US Commission has examined the adequacy of the existing legal provisions for collective bargaining and employee participation.

Collective Bargaining

Collective bargaining is a process that aims at balancing the two basically unequal forces with their inherent clash of interests. Certain legal provisions are essential to facilitate this process. The basic precondition of freedom of association is required to be coupled with a preventive precondition for employers to interfere with this right of employees. Similarly the right not to associate should also be protected. The Wagner Act of 1935 (National Labour Relations Act) and the Taft Hartley Act of 1947 conferred both these rights on workers in the US. Supervisors, managers, agricultural workers and domestic workers are excluded from the coverage of these laws.

Union elections are conducted by the National Labour Relations Board (NLRB). The Commission has noted that from

1975 to 1990, the number of elections fell by 55 per cent. The hearing before the Commission revealed that the design and administration of the National Labour Relations Act (NLRA) are not conducive to providing workers a free choice about union representation. More than illegal actions of some employers, the 'veiled threat and act of discrimination which cannot be proven to be unlawfully motivated' are responsible for workers keeping away from unionization. It has been found that in one in every four elections, improper dismissals of union activists takes place. The Commission has recommended that the union elections should be held promptly; within two weeks of receiving a petition by the parties. Second, it recommended that the NLRB be empowered to give immediate injunctive relief against discriminatory actions. In the event of a dispute, the Commission recommended a flexible dispute resolution of first contract negotiations including arbitration where necessary.

Employee Participation

The importance of employee participation in management for a cohesive atmosphere at the workplace is beyond any doubt. The US scenario on this front is rather confusing even for the Commission. This confusion arises from the dichotomy that on the one hand a large number of employees and employers seem to have realized the importance of participation. Also, the proportion of organizations using some form of participation varies between one-fifth to one-third of all organizations. Yet, on the other hand, evidence also shows that the survival rate of these participation programmes is very low. The Commission refers to some surveys which revealed that only in about one-third of such establishments the employee participation programmes have continued for five or more years. The survival rate of quality circles, too, is very low.

The Commission has observed that these participation programmes will be sustained if the union is involved as a joint partner. This observation has come in the wake of some managements taking an initiative in setting up employee committees by *nominating* some employees as representatives. These were *not elected* by the membership. This was in clear violation of the National Labour Relations Act.

In the Commission's opinion, employees are apathetic to participation schemes due to a lack of trust in the management. It has noted that the workers' biggest apprehension was that participation would result in loss of their jobs. Alternately, the supervisors and managers keep away from such schemes because they are denied the right to unionize and hence they fear victimization by management. Workers who are given supervisory responsibilities in participation schemes have to forego legal protection and hence can be dismissed easily. In view of this, the Commission has recommended that 'the Congress should simplify and restrict the supervisory and managerial employee exclusion of the NLRA to ensure that the vast numbers of professionals and other workers who wish to participate in decision-making at work are not stripped of their right to do so through collective bargaining if they so choose' (p. 9 Report and Recommendations). The Commission further recommended that the definition of supervisor and manager should be updated and that they should not be excluded from participation programmes.

Despite the noble objective of participation, the schemes of employee participation have lost their popularity and effectiveness in USA. Interestingly, the experience in Britain and India has been similar despite cultural and socio-economic differences. As for Britain, Roderick Martin (1981)[16] notes,

The history of joint institution, whether consultation or participation in British industrial relations as a whole...has not been encouraging. Although joint institutions have been successfully established, their practical effects have been limited...lower level joint institutions dealing with more detailed issues have succeeded only in limited areas such as training or working as industry pressure groups.... Except for a very small minority of firms with a principled commitment to joint institutions, the scope of joint decision-making at company and plant level has been restricted, usually to welfare and safety issues' (p. 200).

Unlike in the USA, the supervisors and managers in the UK and India do not live in the shadow of dismissal due to their participation in joint councils. However, as Hanson (1994)[17] notes '...(schemes of participation are) seen (by the middle management) as an arrangement by which top management communicates directly with office and/or works staff, bypassing intermediate managers and supervisors. Nothing is more likely to undermine the authority and damage the morale of middle managers and supervisor....' (p. 162). In Indian industries too, this researcher has come across similar feelings expressed by the middle cadre employees.

Indian and British workers enjoy full legal protection which does not come in the way of their participation. The case with supervisors has been similar. But in India, their real problem has been non-recognition by management. Their earnings, too, are lower than the workers due to the latter's entitlement for overtime wages, bonus and incentive earnings. This makes the middle cadre employees lose interest in jobs and alienates them from their work and organization.

All schemes of participation, everywhere, have shown a trend of downward enthusiasm and total disinterest. The Involvement and Participation Association (IPA) of UK observed in its document on Industrial Partnership (1992) that 'The key element in consultation is not the machinery by which it happens but the subjects on which managements are prepared to consult with employees or their representatives and the style used'.[18] Issues covered in schemes of participation are determined by the level at which participation takes place. Decisions pertaining to capital investment and product diversification can never be a subject of worker participation unless there is employee shareholding, profit-sharing and board level participation. Till such time as it materializes, employees will be treated as both human assets (due to an increased awareness about human resource management) and production factors.

The obvious anomaly in these two approaches (i.e., human asset and labour cost) can be reduced by participation schemes. It must be accepted, however, that these schemes cannot bring about magical results. But the least that they can do is check the feeling of hatred and move towards building a team spirit. The US Commission's recommendations, too, are required to be taken in the same spirit.

Various developments in industrial relations practices the world over have come about after the economics of labour unrest became detrimental to the very existence of business. The realization that modernization can succeed only with cohesive industrial relations has transformed the managements' approach towards employees. This transformation has been summed up in the next chapter.

REFERENCES

1. **D. R. Gadgil**, *Industrial Evolution in India in Recent Times*, Oxford University Press, 1938, pp. 286–87.
2. **David Coats**, *The Crisis of Labour: Industrial Relations and the State in Contemporary Britain*, Philip Allan, 1989, p. 170.

3. **Ken Coats** and **Tony Topham**, *Trade Unions in Britain*, Spokesman, 1980, p. 217.

4. **Manik Kher**, 'Trade Unionism in the Nineties in India: Deunionization', a paper presented at the IX World Congress of the International Industrial Relations Association held in Sydney in 1992.

5. **F. Herzberg, B. Mausner** and **B. Snyderman**, *The Motivation to Work*, John Wiley and Sons, 1959, p. 15.

6. **John Bessant**, 'Towards Factory 2000: Designing Organizations for Computers Integrated Technologies', in *Human Resource Management and Technical Change*, ed. Jon Clark, Sage, 1993, pp. 192–211.

7. **Peter Hain**, *Political Strikes*, Penguin, 1986, p. 308.

8. **Charles G. Hanson**, *Taming the Trade Unions*, Macmillan, in association with the Adam Smith Institute, 1994, p. 157.

9. See p. 31 in supra 7.

10. **Philip Bassett**, *Strike Free: New Industrial Relations in Britain*, Macmillan, 1986, p. 154.

11. **Gregor Gall** and **Sonia Mckay**, 'Trade Union Derecognition in Britain 1988–1994', in *British Journal of Industrial Relations*, Vol. 32, No. 3, 1994, pp. 433–48.

12. **J. Storey**, Cited in *Technological Change at Work*, eds: Ian Mcloughlin and Jon Clark, Open University Press, 1994. p. 72.

13. **Ian Mcloughlin** and **Jon Clark**, 'Technological Change at Work in Comparative Perspective' in supra 12, pp. 208–33.

14. **Saul Rubinstein, Michael Bennett** and **Thomas Kochan**, 'The Saturn Partnership: Co-Management and the Reinvention of the local Union'.

15. **U.S. Department of Labour**, *Fact Finding Report of The Commission on the Future of Worker-Management Relations*, May and December 1994.

16. **Roderick Martin**, *New Technology and Industrial Relations in Fleet Street*, Oxford, 1981, p. 200.

17. **Charles G. Hanson**, supra 8, p. 162.

18. As quoted by Taylor Robert in *The Future of the Trade Unions*, André Deutsch, 1994, p. 201.

10

Summing Up

The foregoing chapters were aimed at analysing the entire process of modernization from various angles with a focus on industrial relations. Their overview once again reiterates the issue that despite various odds, we cannot turn our backs on new technology. In diverse ways of modernizing work processes and the resultant trade union–management dynamics across industries and regions, the managerial objectives stand out very clearly as a common denominator. They adopt new technology in order to produce high quality goods at a reduced cost with improved efficiency and profitability. Technological inputs reduce the cycle time of production and thereby bring down the operating costs comprising energy, labour and raw material. Proper implementation of an upgraded technology gives a higher yield because of the tremendous reduction in re-work and wastages.

Technological change can bring rich dividends if it is timely and implemented with a lot of care and concern about employee cooperation. It was seen that on this front the public sector lagged far behind the private sector. Employees need to be taken into confidence before initiating the change. They require to be trained, and above all, a technology friendly work culture must prevail for a successful modernization process. Its implementation varied across the 22 companies covered in this study.

Technological change means different things to different people. Of these, its effect on employment is of primary concern to policy-makers, academia and trade unions. From the business point of view, technological change has different implications altogether. The lessons emerging from the study will be analyzed separately in the next chapter. The overall and long-term impact of new technology on industrial relations is now discussed.

Technological upgradation increasingly takes over the human skill and effort and the content of manual labour. The labour displacing effect of new technology is considered its biggest drawback. Against the backdrop of the existing level of unemployment, new technology is viewed as a social threat because of its lower potential to generate employment. But the bitter truth is that despite such side-effects, acceptance of new technology has no substitute. Its role in sustaining a business as well as promoting its competitive edge is beyond any doubt. Delays in modernization in the public sector on account of the concomitant threats of labour redundancy, union opposition, lack of funds and bureaucratic policies have proved to be harmful to the economic health of the nation.

Over time, unions have realized the inevitability of modern-ization. While they do not reject the new technology outright, they seem to obstruct its implementation merely in order to increase their margin in the 'price for acceptance'.

This change in union approaches has to be understood in the wake of the deindustrialization in West Bengal (due to growing labour militancy during the seventies) followed by the wave of violent trade unionism in Bombay in the late seventies and the textile strike in the early eighties. These sent sharp signals to both the labour unions and managements across the country. As a result, the collective bargaining process has undergone a change. There is an increasing thrust towards bipartite settlements with the nominal endorsement by the labour commissioner in order to safeguard legally its binding effect. The process of give and take during negotia-tions has become prominent as never before. Trade unions' responsibilities are reiterated and work discipline is enforced through the counter-demands of managements.

Workers in the organized and unionized sector have pros-pered. Long-drawn strikes are a thing of the past due to fear of an economic set-back. While they do maintain their union membership (in view of the calculated advantages), they seem to have lost interest in union activities and, as such, long-drawn strikes are a thing of the past. Union leaders admit poor turnout at the meetings and other activities. Moreover, they have to even pester members to pay the union subscription. The original political ideologies linked with the unions are no longer their binding force. With the rising level of education and awareness among workers, union leaders have lost their power to shape workers' opinions about the political situation. Hence the leaders admit that they cannot guarantee workers' support to the political parties to which their unions are affiliated.

With the increased investment in sophisticated and capital intensive technology and the intense market competition, managements cannot afford work stoppages due to labour unrest. This has forced them to treat workers not merely as a component of capital, but also as 'human resource'. They have innovated many goodwill practices varying from sending a birthday card to an employee to organizing family visits to the company. The increased level of automation has also compelled the managements to provide job enrichment through various participatory forums, training, multi-skills and job rotation. This will have a very positive effect on creating harmony.

Another major impact of modernization on collective bargaining has been that it is shifting from industry-based bargaining to firm-based bargaining. This has been observed especially in the case of the textile industry. As and when the mills are being modernized, unions are bargaining on the basis of the firm's capacity to pay rather than signing a common settlement for all mills. The steel industry may move in the same direction. However, this may not be possible in the engineering industry mainly on account of the vastness in size and the varied operations.

The principle of wage bargaining on the basis of capacity to pay will also create more wage disparities across sectors and industries. This trend has already set in with the entry of multinational companies. Besides, companies seem to be 'buying peace' at any cost. Indian companies will find it difficult to keep pace with the current trend of the galloping increase in the compensation packages in order to retain their employees and attract fresh ones. This will further contribute to inflation. An incomes policy alone will help keep the inflation under control.

The world over the process of industrialization and its intensification with sophisticated technology has changed the composition of employment across economic sectors. There has been a shift from agriculture to industry and from industry to the tertiary sector. In India, however, this trend is seen only at the micro level of the large unionized industries. But at the macro level, as seen in the following data, this has not happened.

In the organized sector, especially at the micro level, this researcher did come across the suspension in recruitment of rank and file workers due to automation. The strength of the middle management employees in these companies has risen due to the increased need of services in sales, marketing and computerization. However, at the macro level, as can be observed from Table 10.1, the tertiary sector has outgrown the manufacturing sector only marginally. The tertiary sector has grown by 2.8 per cent over the two census periods. Employment in the manufacturing sector during the same period has come down by 0.9 per cent. In the primary sector the same has come down by 2.1 per cent during the same decade.

At the micro level of the large unionized sector, as an obvious and a combined impact of technological change and ever-rising labour costs, there is an increasing thrust on subcontracting of jobs (also known as outsourcing) to the smaller firms in the informal sector. The large industries have been manufacturing only the value-added products.

We have noted in chapter seven that despite increasing wages combined with good facilities, across all sectors, industries and regions, there is a tremendous lack of work culture. In fact this defect seems to have acquired a national character. Various unproductive work practices do hamper productivity and retard the growth of economic development. Managements and unions should strive to educate employees and the general public towards inculcating the value of good and disciplined work.

The preceding chapters have also highlighted that the effectiveness of all innovative management practices such as the Total Quality Management, Just-in-Time, Kaizen and Re-engineering ultimately depends upon work culture as well as an

TABLE 10.1

Employment across Sectors

(Figures in Millions)

Sector	1991	1981
Primary Sector		
1. Cultivators	107.1	91.5
	(38.4)	(41.5)
2. Agricultural Labourers	73.8	55.4
	(26.4)	(25.1)
3. Livestock, forestry, fishing, plantations and		
allied activities	5.3	5.0
	(1.9)	(2.2)
4. Mining and quarrying	1.7	1.3
	(0.6)	(0.6)
Secondary Sector		
5. Manufacturing, processing, servicing etc.	28.4	24.9
	(10.2)	(11.3)
of which: in household industry	6.7	7.6
	(2.4)	(3.5)
6. Construction	5.4	3.7
	(1.9)	(1.7)
Tertiary Sector		
7. Trade and Commerce	20.8	14.0
	(7.5)	(6.3)
8. Transport, storage and communication	7.8	6.1
	(2.8)	(2.8)
9. Other services	28.5	18.9
	(10.2)	(8.6)
Total Main Workers (1–9)	278.9	220.7
	(100.0)	(100.0)

Source: Statistical Outline of India, 1994–95.

Note: Figures in parentheses indicate percentages to total. The data exclude the states of Assam and Jammu and Kashmir.

efficient Human Resource Management. The latter manifests itself in open communication, closely knit cross-functional teams, flatter organizational structures, a customer-oriented approach with a cohesive work atmosphere within the organization.

This can be best achieved by combining all schemes of participation in decision-making with that of employee stock option schemes. Financial stakes should explicitly impose responsibilities also for losses and damages caused due to destruction of machinery and the infrastructure during the period of labour unrest. Participation in decision-making and in various activities of joint endeavour between unions and managements without a share in profits/losses, would lead the workers to take irrational decisions with selfish and short-term interests. Similarly, participation merely in profits/losses without a voice in the decision-making process at all levels would provoke workers to blame the management on some pretext or the other. Hence, participation at both levels cannot be separated. Imposition of financial responsibility alone would create voluntary checks on the dysfunctions of various activities.

Is it possible to create a workers' cooperative and totally eradicate the feelings of 'us' and 'them'? Experiences of the communist countries have proved to be contrary to an optimistic expectation. As noted in the previous chapter, an Indian experiment in worker ownership too ended in failure.

In India, there is a tremendous educational gap even between a highly skilled worker and a manager. Yet when given opportunities and training, workers are found to have overcome this drawback. They have even contributed to technological innovation and shopfloor management. Hence, when accompanied with financial participation and account-ability, a technology friendly work atmosphere conducive to modernization and profitability will emerge, it is hoped.

From this analysis it is possible to draw some inferences for managements. These are presented in the next chapter.

175

11

Lessons for Management

The modernization plan essentially centres around three aspects. (*a*) Technology (*b*) Systems and (*c*) People. These are at once interconnected as well as directly related to the implementation of new technology. The managerial responsibilities pertaining to these are now analyzed.

TECHNOLOGY

Choice of technology is a highly specialized task encompassing the technical expertise related to machinery and product, law, finance and marketing. It essentially calls for a coordinated effort of the managerial team. By and large, Indian managers lack such team spirit. It needs to be cultivated through a conscious effort by organizing sessions on sensitivity training, transactional analysis and organizational development. Teamwork is possible only in a friendly atmosphere free from suspicion. Any lapse in coordinated teamwork would result in the delayed launching of the modernization programme, under-utilization of capacity and, above all, a prolonged period of return on investment.

Technological change is basically an exercise in re-engineering. It is a continuous task of self-introspection for improving quality, cutting costs, reducing the cycle time of production and delivery time, product development and diversification. The ultimate aim of all these is customer satisfaction: the key element in a market economy.

Safety, Health and Environment (SHE)

An important technology oriented function of management relates to three features, commonly known as the SHE factor comprising Safety, Health and Environment. These are inseparable from each other and constitute the social responsibility of business. This responsibility is now enunciated in various statutes such as the Water (Prevention and Control of Pollution Act), 1974, the Air (Prevention and Control of Pollution Act), 1981 and the Environment Protection Act, 1986.

Safety, like quality and productivity, forms an integral part of the organizational culture and the core function of management. Managements should train employees on safety matters. Any lapse in observing safety precautions should not be overlooked. Managements tend to ignore the incidence of workers reporting to work without safety shoes, safety goggles, masks and safety belts. More often than not, safety equipment is given only to permanent employees leaving out a large number of contract labour. The nature of employment has nothing to do with vulnerability and accident-proneness and as such managements should ensure that contractors fulfill their obligations towards the safety of the contract labour at work.

Health and environment go hand in hand. Setting up of effluent treatment plants is still confined only to the large and medium sectors. The small sector finds them unaffordable. As a unique experiment, a large chemical company near Mumbai (Bombay) has been building a common effluent treatment plant, apart from its own, where the small-scale units will send their effluents for treatment at a nominal fee. Many of the treated effluents can be reused for the afforestation programme. What is required is the management willingness to undertake such a social obligation.

SYSTEMS

The word systems is all pervasive; encompassing all functions of management. All systems and procedures should orient from customer needs, customer satisfaction and employee motivation.

Technological change demands restructuring and re-organizing of hierarchical levels, functions and people. Restructuring is best organized when centred around products and services. The problems of inefficiency on various counts emerge from inadequate communication, lack of sound infrastructure and flexibility. Managements need to develop an efficient management information system which facilitates timely checks on quality and continuity of various inputs and outputs.

Maintenance

Increased level of automation has made managements realize the value of maintenance which was long neglected. Maintenance systems need to be planned much prior to the arrival of new machinery on the shopfloor. Maintenance is a function of not the employees in the maintenance department alone, but also of each and every person involved in manufacturing operations.

PEOPLE

For making modernization a success, the work atmosphere should be infused with 'learned willingness and individual accountability' to borrow the words of James Champy.[1] This is possible only if the management and employees trust each other. Creating trust requires a continuous and long-term perseverance on the part of management. We have seen how the coffee meetings and the state of the business meetings of a CEO in an engineering company in the south helped restore trust among employees. The CEO's action was induced by the thought that 'if the shareholders of the company could have the right to information, why not the employees?' When trust was restored through such openness in information-sharing, employees volunteered themselves to clean the shopfloor when it was flooded with mud and rain water and due to which the management had declared its inability to continue operations. Ricardo Semler,[2] the owner-executive of SEMCO, acknowledged to be the best in Brazil has given an interesting account of how he improved communication through weekly meetings. He introduced three key elements in order to improve his relations with employees. These are: democracy, transparency and trust. Managers need to develop a strong commitment towards these values.

Similarly Robert Frey,[3] the owner-president of CinMade Corporation notes how he induced his managers to share more information with employees. He began using these meetings 'to make profit projections,...examine scrap rates and materials prices and operation efficiencies'.

EMPLOYEE EMPOWERMENT

The recent concept of Employee Empowerment is nothing but making an employee feel important and powerful. Information-sharing is the first step on the path of empowerment. Any scheme of employee participation cannot be meaningful unless the management is honest in sharing all kinds of information about the organization. As noted in the previous chapter, all forms of participation can be effective if coupled with financial participation.

Managerial functions are founded on the reliability of employees. It is only the motivated workforce which can be reliable and trustworthy. Hence managements should consider it their prime responsibility to keep the employees motivated. Basic to motivation is the feeling of being recognized by management. Recognition can be given not merely through a promotion and wage increment but also by publicizing achievements and good work through notice boards, bulletins, meetings and annual functions.

Managements need to be fair to employees in performance appraisals. The criteria for evaluating their performance should be made known to them.

While considering these positive aspects, one cannot ignore the negative aspects concerning the work behaviour. When unproductive work practices are followed many managements tend to adopt a soft approach due to fear of unions. Instead of hushing up such indiscipline, they should communicate it immediately not only to the erring employee but also to his team members and union representatives. Self-discipline is possible only when employees are honest. Values of honesty and trustworthiness cannot be internalized unless the managers themselves set a good example to this effect. Managements need to make relentless efforts to inculcate self-discipline among employees and improve work culture.

Any organizational activity, including modernization, can be successful if an optimum equilibrium is achieved between technology, systems and people. This can be best incorporated in one single yet the most challenging objective propounded by Semler: To make people look forward to coming to work the next morning.

REFERENCES

1. **James Champy**, *Reengineering Management: The Mandate for New Leadership*, Harper Collins, 1995.
2. **Ricardo Semler**, *Maverick!* Arrow, 1993.
3. **Robert Frey**, 'Empowerment or Else' as reproduced from *Harvard Business Review* in *The Times of India*, (ASCENT), 2 October 1995.

Statistical Appendix

I. Textile Industry—1992–93
(All India)

Mill Sector
1. No. of mills

Type	Public (NTC)	Cooperative	Private	Total
Spinning	74	118	679	871
Composite	114	2	155	271
Total	188	120	834	1142
	(16.5)	(10.50)	(73.0)	(100.0)

Note: 10 lakhs: 1 million; 1 crore: 10 million

2. Installed capacity (000)

Type	Public (NTC)	Cooperative	Private	Total
Spindles	6040	2970	18920	27930
	(21.6)	(10.6)	(67.8)	(100.0)
Rotors	1.21	5.52	109.80	116.53
	(1.1)	(4.7)	(94.2)	(100.0)
Looms	70.59	0.29	97.64	168.52
	(41.9)	(0.2)	(57.9)	(100.0)

3. Total no. of workers (lakhs)

Public	Cooperative	Private	Total
2.78	1.01	6.77	10.56
(26.3)	(9.5)	(64.2)	(100.0)

B. 1. Closure of mills

	1991–92	1992–93
Spinning	68	64
Composite	62	58
	130	122

2. Idle capacity due to closure (000)

	1991–92	1992–93	% to total
Spindles	3823	3567	12.77
Rotors	2.9	1.18	1.1
Looms	40.9	36.2	21.48

3. Workers affected (lakhs)

	1991–92	1992–93	% to total
	1.94	1.72	16.29

C. Capacity Utilization

Spindles	Maximum	80 per cent in 1990–91
	Actual	55 per cent in 1992–93
Looms	Maximum	65 per cent in 1988–89
	Actual	55 per cent in 1992–93

D. Production of Fabrics (Lakh sq.metres). 1992–93

			Proportion
1.	Mills	20,140	8.68
2.	Handlooms	41,950	18.08
3.	Powerlooms including hosiery	1,65,780	71.48
4.	Khadi	4,060	1.76
		2,31,930	100.00

The powerlooms sector has been dominating and is growing strong. It rose from 55.52 per cent in 1988–89 to 71.48 per cent in 1992–93.

No. of *resgistered* powerlooms: 12.92 lakhs; giving direct employment to about 60 lakh persons.

Covered under the Research Project

A. Two Mills (Profit-making)

	1989–90	*1992–93*
1. Installed capacity		
Spindles (000)	315.77	270.58
Looms	4.34	2.98
Rotors	1.54	4.22

(a) Change in production lines from cloth and yarn to electronics, and new textile products for exports.

(b) Though the installed capacity of spindles is reduced, production of cloth in one mill and yarn in another has increased owing to technological improvement in one mill.

(c) Though reduction in waste is one of the objectives of technological improvement, its production is on the rise.

B. Production

	1989–90	1992–93
1. Cloth (lakh sq.metres)	1840.39	1903.66
2. Yarn (lakh kgs.)	16.33	20.77
3. Waste (lakh kgs.)	71.80	80.39

C. Consumption per unit of production

1. Electricity : 0.8 KWH per metre to 1.98 KWH per metre (No distinctive reduction)
2. Coal : 0.806 Kg. per metre of cloth (No distinctive reduction)

D. Proportion of Exports to Total Sales

Increased from 15.83 per cent in 1987–88 to 25.13 per cent in 1992–93. (Export-oriented change in production and technology).

Two sick mills (loss-making)

	1989–90	1992–93
I. Installed capacity		
Spindles (000)	124.0	144.0
Looms (000)	1.8	2.1
II. Production		
Cloth (lakh metres)	345.12	289.96
Yarn (lakh kgs.)	8.06	9.14
(Yarn production in one mill increased)		
In closing stocks of cloth (lakh metres)	231.27	118.50
III. Accumulated loss		
Rs. (crores)	115.36	222.07
IV. Proportion of liabilities to assets	192%	284%

N.T.C. mills (Based on data made available)

9 (Regions in India) = 9 subsidiaries of NTC

A.	1989	Crores
Total assets		836.08
Total production		828.15
Total wages		321.91
Total loss		235.96
Cumulative loss (1980–81)		1206.50

Wages 136.42 per cent of loss
Profits in 4 regions only in 1980 and 1981.
All assets wiped out

B.	1992–93	Crores
Total assets		1195.01
Accumulated loss		2439.28
Sales revenue		899.86
Employee remuneration		381.06
Loss (1992–93)		570.54

Employee remuneration as percentage 42.35 % to sales
Employee remuneration as percentage 66.79 % to loss

N.T.C. (visited) Bombay

Maharashtra (North)	1991–92
1. Installed capacity	
Spindles	2,63,096
(Reduced from 392796 in 1974–75)	
Looms	4,911
(Reduced from 8612 in 1974–75)	
2. Production	
1. Controlled cloth (lakh metres)	199.93
2. Non-controlled cloth (lakh metres)	744.28
	944.21

3. Maximum production
   1. Controlled cloth in 1980–81   1124.58
           lakh metres
   2. Non-controlled cloth in 1974–75   1474.92
           lakh metres
3. Operatives employed per day   12739
   (Reduced from 24233 in 1974–75)
4. (a) Workers per 1000 spindle shift   5.43
   (b) Workers per 100 loom shift   50.90
5. Nett loss   Rs. 23.97 crores
6. Cumulative loss from 1974–75 to 1991–92   Rs. 263.59 crores

N.T.C. (Gujarat), Ahmedabad

Out of 10 composite mills and 1 knitting mill nationalised on 1–4–1974, 7 mills virtually stopped working by January 1993.

	1992–93
1. Installed capacity	
Spindles	296656
Looms	6013
2. Cumulative loss	Rs. 317.21 crores
(From 1974–75 to 1992–93)	
3. Own capital of Rs. 261.97 crores wiped out completely.	
Liabilities Rs. 92.16 crores (Dues)	
4. (a) Total No. of workers of which already relieved	17537
up to 1–8–1993 under V.R.S.	6396
	11141
(b) Of which Badli	3588
(Those who have completed 240 days—2776).	
(c) Found surplus as on 1–9–1993 in 3 working mills	2205
Of which likely to opt for VRS	1111
Net surplus in 3 mills	1094

5. Modernization plan for 8 mills costing Rs.124.87 crores, could absorb 3664 workers rendering 2513 employees surplus.
6. Production value 1992–93   Rs. 63.91 crores
   Employee remuneration 1992–93   Rs. 45.13 crores
7. Proportion of employee remuneration to net loss for the years 1986–87 to 1992–93

                                  ... 117.98%

N.T.C. (Tamil Nadu and Pondicherry), Coimbatore

Spinning mills and 7 composite mills

1. Installed capacity	1993–94
Spindles	489792
Rotors	360
Looms	856
2. Production	
Cloth (lakh metres)	201.0
Yarn (lakh kgs.)	242.0
3. (i) Sales	Rs. 292.17 crores
(ii) Exports	Rs. 20.20 crores
Proportion of (ii) to (i)	6.91%
4. (i) No. of employees	12340
(ii) Per day average	10362
5. Gross profit	Rs. 24.32 crores

(Only Regional NTC Corporation showing profits)
6. 2197 employees (of which 2103 workers) opted for VRS from 1987–88 to 1993–94 and were paid Rs. 11.25 crores.
7. Modernization continuous—so far invested Rs. 147.35 crores.

ENGINEERING COMPANIES

Private Limited Companies did not provide their Annual Reports. Hence the following data relate to those companies covered in the project and those which gave such Reports.

(Rs. Crores)

	1988–89	1992–93
1. Capital		
Share capital	111.78	138.87
Internal resources	341.68	727.55
Loans	369.34	1561.98
	822.80	2428.40
2. Sales	1824.99	3295.40
3. Expenditure		
1. Payments to employees	213.95	347.13
2. Interest	67.09	234.80
3. Depreciation	47.66	86.25
4. Mfg. expenses	1440.74	2806.83
5. Royalty	0.55	2.53
	1769.99	3477.54
4. Expenditure on R & D	12.71	94.39
Percentage to total turnover	0.75	3.75
5. Value of exports	83.78	345.11
6. Imports (Including capital goods)	76.19	165.99
7. Royalty fees	0.55	2.53
8. Percentage of imported raw materials to total consumption.	19.54	15.83

Engineering Industries

A. One multinational company merged with a foreign company

1. Class of goods manufactured
   a. Dairy machinery and equipment (11.5)
   b. Stainless steel fittings, pumps and refrigeration
      plants. (8.6)
   c. Oil separators, vaccum units (28.2)
   d. Food, beverages and food processing plants (8.8)
   e. Equipments for chemical, pharmaceutical and
      other allied industries (3.5)
   f. Biostil and yeast recycling plants (9.4)
   g. Others (30.0)

(Figures in brackets indicate proportion in sales, i.e. importance in the class of goods manufactured).

(Rs. in Crores)

	1986	1992–93
2. Capital		
a. Share capital	5.22	18.16
b. Internal resources generated	15.07	93.50
c. Loan funds	8.23	35.11
	28.52	146.77
3. Sales	46.21	162.80
4. Profits before tax	2.45	23.79
5. a. Mfg. expenses	44.39	136.75
b. Depreciation	0.73	1.67
c. Interest	1.33	5.28
Total of (5)	46.45	143.70

(a) Mfg. expenses of which

	Rs.	Rs.
(i) Payments to employees	4.61	12.53 (9%)
(ii) Sub-contractors' charges	0.89	4.90 (3.6%)
(iii) Technical knowhow fees	0.60	1.80 (1.3%)
(iv) Royalty	0.19	0.18 (0.1%)

7.	Proportion of imported raw material consumed to total consumption of raw materials	35.9%	33.0%
8.	Foreign exchange earned	6.96	14.91
9.	Remittances		
	(i) Raw material	7.89	17.80
	(ii) Capital goods	0.17	1.83
	(iii) Technical fees and royalty and knowhow fees	1.61	1.86
	(iv) Dividend	0.12	0.88
	(v) Others	0.20	0.53
		9.99	22.90

10. Expenditure on R&D

	1988–89	*1992–93*
(i) Capital	0.04	2.72
(ii) Others	0.56	0.51
	0.60	3.23
	About 1% of total turnover	About 2% of total turnover

One Public Sector Company established in 1952

1. Manufacturing of cables (91.80%), wires (2.80%), and undertaking turnkey projects (1.52%).
   [Figures in brackets indicate percentages to total value of production]

(Rs. Crores)

	1989–90	*1992–93*
2. Capital		
a. Paid up capital	45.83	82.33
b. Internal resources generated	75.03	66.05
c. Loan funds	233.37	383.15
3. Value of production	339.69	414.20

4. Sales	408.56	522.76
5. Profit before tax	7.91	12.11
6. Manufacturing expenses		
a. Mfg. expenses	358.75	413.35
b. Employees' remuneration	32.83	41.62
c. Depreciation	17.14	15.97
d. Interest	32.72	46.08
	441.44	517.02

7. No. of employees	7134	7012
(Reduced from 7145 in 1990–91) of which in 1992–93		
Physically handicapped	75	
SC/ST	1584	
Ex-servicemen	280	
	1939	

8. Foreign exchange earned	Nil
9. Foreign remittances	

	Rs.
(i) Raw material	61.11
(ii) Capital goods	47.35
(iii) Consultation fees	0.20
(iv) Interest and dividend	1.88
(v) Others	0.20
	110.74

10. Expenditure on R & D

	1989–90	1992–93
(i) Capital	–	0.05
(ii) Recurring	1.67	1.01
	1.67	1.06
	0.20% of total turnover	

STEEL INDUSTRY

1. Six integrated steel plants
   SAIL – Bhilai, Bokaro, Durgapur, Rourkela
   IISCO
   TISCO
2. Financial details of one private limited company not available.

(Rs. Crores)

	1989–90			1993–94	
	Six integrated plants	Of which One Pvt. Ltd. Co.	One Public Ltd. Co.	Another Public Ltd. Co.	Same Pvt. Ltd. Co.
1. Capital					
Share capital	4597.26	216.19	229.43	6527.54	335.21
Resources and Surplus	1913.85	0.31	1103.11	–	2189.53
Loans	5645.46	357.01	954.11	3613.39	3428.59
	12156.57	573.51	2286.65	10140.93	5953.33
2. Sales	9866.66	696.69	1976.16	1751.03	3790.97
3. Expenditure					
1. Payment to employees	1452.96	155.93	354.01	102.49	590.54
2. Interest	428.62	21.28	117.24	346.44	199.28
3. Depreciation	676.88	36.66	118.79	328.53	177.70
4. Mfg. Expenses	7815.14	698.43	1435.04	1528.52	3395.70
	10373.60	912.30	2025.08	2305.98	4363.22
4. Profit after tax	200.91	(–)94.85	148.53	(–)559.12	180.84
5. Royalty	NOT APPLICABLE				58.87

6. Expenditure on R&D (capital and recurring)	2.5	10.50
7. Percentage to total turnover	0.131	0.3
8. Value of exports	589.39	708.68
9. Imports (including capital goods)	419.72	356.30
10. Percentage of imported raw materials to total consumption	42.72	15.89
11. Expenditure on technical know-how and technical consultants fees (in foreign currency)	27.14	28.24

	1989–90 (000 tonnes)	1992–93 (000 tonnes)
1. Production		
(i) Saleable steel		
a. Six integrated steel plants	9029	11338
b. One Public Ltd.	700	641
c. One Private Ltd.	1966	2124
d. Greenfield Public Ltd.	–	879
2. Non-Executive Personnel at Works/Plants		
a. Six integrated steel plants	2,45,792	2,18,380 (+12390)
b. One Public Ltd.	18,718	19,413
c. One Private Ltd.	29,920	33,881
d. Greenfield Public Ltd.	–	12,390
3. Labour Productivity (Works Personnel) Ingot tonnes per Man-year		
a. One Public Ltd.	42	34
b. One Private Ltd.	74	72
c. Greenfield Public Ltd.	–	110

	1992–93

4. No. of Persons Trained at the Steel Plants

    a. Two Public Ltd. Cos.   19359
    b. One Private Ltd.   13563

5. No.of Persons Trained Abroad

    a. Two Public Ltd.   190
    b. One Private Ltd.   147

6. Profit and Loss

    a. One Public Ltd. Co.- Loss continues to be increased since inception in 1959–60, rose from 8.70 crores in 1961–62 to Rs 90.32 crores in 1991–92. (Accumulated loss Rs 878.02 crores).

    b. Greenfield Public Ltd. Co. (full-fledged working since 1992–93
    Profit   Rs. 55'4.78 crores
    Loss 1993–94   Rs. 559.12 crores
    (Accumulated loss   Rs.2605.43 crores)

    c. Private Ltd. Co.
    Continuous profits since inception in 1915–16.
    Rose from Rs. 47.65 crores in 1981–82 to Rs. 180.84 crores in 1992–93.

    Note: Quantum of profits or losses depend on prices of finished products that are fixed by the Government.

7. Consumption (Per tonne of ingot steel)

    Steel Melting Shop

	Public Ltd.		*Pvt. Ltd.*		*Greenfield Public Ltd. Co.*	
	89–90	*92–93*	*89–90*	*92–93*	*89–90*	*92–93*
Heat (10³ K.Cal.)	1121	1056	871	784	138.85	108.91
Electricity (KWH)	30.81	36.23	14.6	12.9	54.45	59.67

8. Investment on social facilities: Proportion of investment on social facilities to total investments (Net block)

   a. One Public Ltd. Co., (1990–91) 14.15%
   b. Another Public Ltd. Co. (1993–94) 3.55%

Excludes expenditure on education, medical, social and cultural activities, cooperatives and transport.

Similar details for the private limited company were not made available (though undertaken by the company).

Bibliography

AILS (Ambedkar Institute of Labour Studies). *Absenteeism—A Case Study in Textile Industry,* Bombay, 1977.

——————. *Research for Trade Unions: A Guide: AILS Experience,* Bombay, 1976–85.

Atkinson, J. 'Manpower Strategies for Flexible Organizations' *Personnel Management* August 1984, pp. 28–29.

Bain, G. S. *Industrial Relations in Britain,* Basil Blackwell, 1983.

Bamber, G. J. and **R. D. Lansbury** (eds). *International and Comparative Industrial Relations,* Allen and Unwin, 1987.

Barnes, D. and **E. Reid.** *Government and Trade Unions: The British Experience 1964–79,* Heinemann, 1980.

Bassett, Philip. *Strike Free: New Industrial Relations in Britain,* Macmillan, 1986.

Batstone, E., S. Gourlay, H. Levie and **R. Moore.** *New Technology and the Process of Labour Regulation,* Clarendon Press, 1987.

Beaumont, P. B. *The Decline of Trade Union Organization,* Crown Helm, 1987.

Bell, D. *The Coming of Post-Industrial Society,* Heinemann, 1974.

Behari, Bepin. *Rural Industrialization in India,* Vikas, 1976.

Benson, I. and **J. Lloyd.** *New Technology and Industrial Change,* Kogan Page, 1983.

Bessant, John. 'Towards Factory 2000: Designing Organizations for Computers—Integrated Technologies' in *Human Resource Management and Technical Change,* (ed.) Jon Clark, Sage, 1993.

Bhagwati, Jagdish. *India in Transition: Freeing the Economy,* Oxford University Press, 1993.

Bhattacharya, D. *A Concise History of Indian Economy,* Progressive, 1970.

Blauner, R. *Alienation and Freedom,* University of Chicago Press, 1964.

Braverman, H. *Labour and Monopoly Capital: The Degradation of Work in the Twentieth Century,* Monthly Review Press, 1974.

Bright, J. *Automation and Management,* Harvard University Press, 1958.

BTRA (Bombay Textile Research Association). *Overall Employment in Textile Industry: Trends in the Last Decade,* SITRA, Coimbatore, 1987.

Brown, W. *The Changing Contours of British Industrial Relations,* Basil Blackwell, 1981.

Bureau of Industrial Costs and Prices. *Report on Comprehensive Study of Integrated Steel Plants in India and International Cost Competitiveness,* Department of Industries, Govt. of India, 1990.

Champy, James. *Reengineering Management: The Mandate for New Leadership,* Harper Collins, 1995.

Chatterjee, R. *Unions, Politics and the State: A Study of Indian Labour Politics,* South Asian Publishers, 1980.

Clegg, H. A. *The Changing System of Industrial Relations in Great Britain,* Blackwell, Oxford, 1979.

Coats, David. *The Crisis of Labour: Industrial Relations and the State in Contemporary Britain,* Philip Allan, 1989.

Coats, Ken and **Tony Topham.** *Trade Unions in Britain,* Spokesman, 1980.

Davies, A. *Industrial Relations and New Technology,* Crown Helm, 1986.

Dawson, S. *Analysing Organizations,* Macmillan, 1986.

Deshpande, L. K. *A Study of Textile Workers on Strike in Bombay,* Centre for the Study of Social Change, Bombay, 1983.

Drucker, Peter. *Post Capitalist Society,* Harper Business, 1994.

Freeman, Chris and **Luc Soete.** *Work for All or Mass Unemployment,* Pinter Publications, 1994.

Frey, Robert. 'Empowerment or Else' as reproduced from *Harvard Business Review* in *The Times of India, (ASCENT)*, 2 October 1995.

Friedman, A. *Industry and Labour*, Macmillan, 1970.

Forester, T. (ed.). *The Information Technology Revolution*, Blackwell, 1985.

Gadgil, D. R. *Industrial Evolution in India in Recent Times*, Oxford University Press, 1938.

Galbraith, John Kenneth. *The New Industrial State*, Oxford & IBH, 1967.

————. *The Anatomy of Power*, Houghton Mifflin, 1983.

Gall, Gregor and **Sonia Mckay.** 'Trade Union Derecognition in Britain 1988–1994', *British Journal of Industrial Relations*, Vol. 32, No. 3. 1994 pp. 433–48.

Ghosh, Alak. *Indian Economy: Its Nature and Problems*, World Press, 1959.

Goswami, Omkar. 'Indian Textile Industry, 1970–1984: An Analysis of Demand and Supply' *Economic and Political Weekly*, Vol. XX, No. 38, 21 September 1985.

Government of India. *Towards an Industrial Democracy*, New Delhi, 1958.

————. *Appropriate Technology for Balanced Regional Development*, New Delhi, Vols. I & II, 1975.

Hain, Peter. *Political Strikes*, Penguin, 1986.

Hanson, Charles G. *Taming the Trade Unions*, Macmillan, 1994.

Herzberg F., B. Mausner and **B. Snyderman.** *The Motivation to Work*, John Wiley and Sons, 1959.

Holmstrom, M. *Industry and Inequality: The Social Anthropology of Indian Labour*, Orient Longman, 1985.

Hyman, R. *The Political Economy of Industrial Relations*, Macmillan, 1988.

Hyman, R. and **W. Streeck** (eds). *New Technology and Industrial Relations*, Blackwell, Oxford.

ILO-ARTEP. *Employment and Structural Change in Indian Industries: A Trade Union View-Point*, New Delhi, 1989.

————. *Social Dimensions of Structural Adjustment in India*, New Delhi, 1992.

Jacobsson, Staffan and **Ghayur Alam.** *Liberalisation and Industrial Development in the Third World: A Comparison of the Indian and South Korean Engineering Industries*, Sage, 1994.

Jawaid, S. *Trade Union Movement in India*, Sundeep Prakashan, 1982.

Jenkins, Clive and **Sherman Barrie.** *The Collapse of Work,* Eyre Methuen, London, 1979.

Juravich, T. *Chaos on the Shopfloor: A Worker's View of Quality, Productivity and Management,* Temple University Press, 1985.

Kaplinsky, R. *Microelectronics and Employment Revisited: A Review,* International Labour Office, Geneva, 1987.

Karnik, V. B. *Indian Trade Unions,* Manaktalas, 1966.

—————. *Strikes in India,* Manaktalas, 1967.

Kelly, John. *Trade Unions and Socialist Policies,* Verso, 1988.

Kher, Manik. 'Trade Unionism in the Nineties in India: Deunionization', a paper presented at the IX World Congress of the International Industrial Relations Association held in Sydney in 1992.

—————. *From Shadows to Light: A Socio-Legal Approach to Work Atmosphere,* The Times Research Foundation, Pune, 1991.

Kher, S. P. 'Relevance of Intermediate Technology' in *Southern Economist,* 1 June 1982.

—————. 'Relevance of Fiscal Incentives for Technological Development' (unpublished mimeo).

Kochan, T., R. Mckersie and **H. Katz.** *The Transformation of American Industrial Relations,* Basic Books, 1986.

Lakshmanna, C., S. P. Srivastava and **R. C. Sarikwal** (eds). *Workers' Participation and Industrial Democracy: Global Perspectives,* Ajanta, 1990.

Lansbury, R. D. and **G. J. Bamber** (eds). *New Technology: International Perspectives on Human Resources and Industrial Relations,* Unwin Hyman, 1989.

Lash, S. and **J. Urry.** *The End of Organized Capitalism,* Polity Press, 1987.

Lawrence, P. and **D. Dyer.** *Renewing American Industry,* Free Press, 1986.

Leadbeater, S. R. B. *The Politics of Textiles: The Indian Cotton-Mill Industry and the Legacy of Swadeshi 1900–1985,* Sage, 1993.

Mani, S. *Foreign Technology in Public Enterprises,* Oxford and IBH Publishing Co., 1992.

Martin, Roderick. *New Technology and Industrial Relations in Fleet Street,* Oxford, 1981.

Mathews, J. *Tools of Change: New Technology and the Democratization of Work,* Pluto Press, 1989.

Mathews, J. *Age of Democracy: The Politics of Post-Fordism,* Oxford University Press, 1989.

Mcloughlin, Ian and **Jon Clark.** *Technological Change At Work*, Open University Press, 1994.

Meade, J. E. *Wage Fixing*, George Allen and Unwin, 1982.

Misra, Sanjiv. *India's Textile Sector: A Policy Analysis*, Sage, 1993.

Mehta, Makrand. *The Ahmedabad Cotton Textile Industry—Genesis and Growth*, New Order Book Co., 1982.

Monger, R. F. *Mastering Technology: A Management Framework for Getting Results*, The Free Press, 1988.

Mortimer, J. E. *Trade Unions and Technological Change*, Oxford University Press, 1971.

Raclin, J. *The Clash of Cultures: Managers and Professionals*, Harvard University Press, 1985.

Rada, J. *The Impact of Microelectronics*, International Labour Office, Geneva, 1980.

Robin, Austin (ed.). *Appropriate Technologies for Third World Development*, St. Martin's Press, 1979.

Rhodes, E. and **D. Weild.** *Implementing New Technologies: Choice, Decision and Change in Manufacturing*, Blackwell, 1985.

Rose, M. *Industrial Behaviour: Research and Control*, Penguin, 1988.

Rubinstein, Saul, Michael Bennett and **Thomas Kochan.** 'The Saturn Partnership: Co-management and the Reinvention of the Local Union'.

Schumacher, E. F. *Small is Beautiful*, Radha Krishna, 1973.

Semler, Ricardo. *Maverick!*, Arrow, 1994.

Sen, Sunil Kumar. *Working Class Movements in India*, Oxford University Press, 1994.

Sisson, K. (ed.). *Personnel Management in Britain*, Blackwell, 1989.

Stoneman, P. *The Economic Analysis of Technological Change*, Oxford University Press, 1983.

Storey, J. *Development in the Management of Human Resources*, Blackwell, 1992.

Tata Economic Consultancy Services. *Industrial Licencing Policy*, Bombay, 1976.

Thompson, P. *The Nature of Work*, Macmillan 1989.

Toffler, A. *The Third Wave*, Pan Books, 1980.

Trade Union Congress. *Employment and Technology*, TUC, London, 1979.

U.S. Department of Labour. *Fact Finding Report of the Commission on the Future of Worker–Management Relations*, May and December 1994.

Van Wersh, H. *The Bombay Textile Strike, 1982–83*, Oxford University Press, 1992.

Vaughan-Whitehead, Daniel, et al. *Workers' Financial Participation: East-West Experience*, ILO, Geneva, 1995.

Willman, Paul. *Technological Change, Collective Bargaining and Industrial Efficiency*, Clarendon Press, 1986.

Wood, S. (ed.). *The Degradation of Work? Skill, Deskilling and the Labour Process*, Hutchinson, 1982.

Woodword, J. (ed.). *Industrial Organization: Behaviour and Control*, Oxford University Press, 1970.

World Bank. *World Development Report*, Oxford, 1995.

Index

Your Response

We want to hear from you!
The details you provide here will help us produce more meaningful books for you and get them to you faster. Kindly fill in the details, cut out this page and return it to: *RESPONSE BOOKS, A division of Sage Publications India Pvt Ltd, Post Box 4215, New Delhi 110 048.*

(please print clearly)
Name: _____ Designation: _____

Address:
Home: _____ Office: _____

_____ _____

_____ _____

Name of the Book: _____

How did you come to hear about this book?

☐ Brochure/catalog ☐ Recommended by a friend/
colleague/teacher/peer

☐ Advertisement in _____ ☐ Other (please elaborate)

_____ _____

☐ Bookstore _____

How did you obtain this book?

☐ Bought it at a bookstore ☐ Borrowed it

☐ Checked it out of the library ☐ Ordered it directly

☐ Other

What do you think of this book?
(please state your views frankly—use an extra sheet if necessary)

_____

_____

What are your areas of interest? (please indicate broad disciplines)

_____

_____

Would you like your name to be included in our mailing list?

☐ No

☐ Yes, enter my home address

☐ Yes, enter my office address

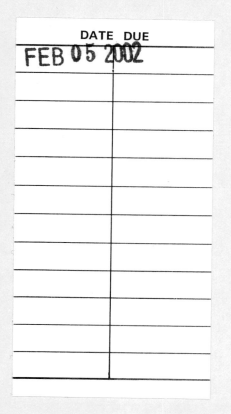